Billy Sunday's Most Powerful Sermons

Volume 1

ISBN-13: 978-1985065321

Dear reader,

Thank you for purchasing *Billy Sunday's Most Powerful Sermons,* Volume 1. These sermons have blessed millions of believers since their original publication, and The New Christian Classics Library is proud to present them to a new generation of believers.

Care has been taken to preserve the original wording, grammar, and vocabulary of this classic text (including items that would be considered typos or errors by today's publishing standards). By doing so, modern readers will be able to experience and enjoy these sermons as countless believers have before them.

Our prayer is that you will benefit from and be challenged by the message herein, and we commit you and your reading of this book to our great God who always answers our prayers above and beyond anything we could think or imagine.

Sincerely,

The New Christian Classics Library

For more Christian classics, visit our Facebook page at:

www.facebook.com/thenewchristianclassicslibrary

Table of Contents

Atonement Through the Blood of Jesus

"For if the blood of bulls and of goats and the ashes of an heifer sprinkling the unclean, sanctifieth to the purifying of the flesh" - Paul argued in his letter to the Hebrews "how much more shall the blood of Christ, who through the eternal Spirit offered himself without spot to God, purge your conscience from dead works to serve the living God."

Hebrews 9:13-14

• • •

No more of this turtle-dove business, no more offering the blood of bullocks and heifers to cleanse from sin.

The atoning blood of Jesus Christ - that is the thing about which all else centers. I believe that more logical, illogical, idiotic, religious and irreligious arguments have been fought over this than all others. Now and then when a man gets a new idea of it, he goes out and starts a new denomination. He has a perfect right to do this under the thirteenth amendment, but he doesn't stop here. He makes war on all of the other denominations that do not interpret as he does. Our denominations have multiplied by this method until it would give one brain fever to try to count them all.

The atoning blood! And as I think it over I am reminded of a man who goes to England and advertises that he will throw pictures on the screen of the Atlantic coast of America. So he gets a crowd and throws pictures on the screen of high bluffs and rocky coasts and waves dashing against them, until a man comes out of the audience and brands him a liar and says that he is obtaining money under false pretense, as he has seen America and the Atlantic coast and what the other man is showing is not America at all. The men almost come to blows and then the other man says that, if the people will come tomorrow, he will show them real pictures of the coast. So the audience comes back to see what he will show, and he flashes on the screen pictures of a low coast line, with palmetto trees and banana trees and tropical foliage and he apologizes to the audience, but says these are the pictures of America. The first man calls him a liar and the people don't know which to believe. What was the matter with them?

They were both right and they were both wrong, paradoxical as it may seem. They were both right as far as they went, but neither went far enough. The first showed the coast line from New England to Cape Hatteras, while the second showed the coast line from Hatteras to Yucatan. They neither could show it all in one panoramic view, for it is so varied it could not be taken in one picture.

God never intended to give you a picture of the world in one panoramic view. From the time of Adam and Eve down to the time Jesus Christ hung on the cross he was unfolding his views. When I see Moses leading the people out of bondage where they for years had bared their backs to the taskmaster's lash; when I see the lowing herds and the high priest standing before the altar severing the jugular vein of the rams and the bullocks; on until Christ cried out from the cross, "It is finished," (John 19:30) God was preparing the picture for the consummation of it in the atoning blood of Jesus Christ.

A sinner has no standing with God. He forfeits his standing when he commits sin and the only way he can get back is to repent and accept the atoning blood of Jesus Christ.

I have sometimes thought that Adam and Eve didn't understand as fully as we do when the Lord said; "Eat and you shall surely die." (Gen. 2:17) They had never seen any one die. They might have thought it simply meant a separation from God. But no sooner had they eaten and seen their nakedness than they sought to cover themselves, and it is the same today. When man sees himself in his sins, uncovered, he tries to cover himself in philosophy or some fake. But God looked through the fig leaves and the foliage and God walked out in the field and slew the beasts and took their skins and wrapped them around Adam and Eve, and from that day to this when a man has been a sinner and has covered himself, it has been by and through faith in the shed blood of Jesus Christ. Every Jew covered his sins and received pardon through the blood of the rams and bullocks and the doves.

An old infidel said to me once, "But I don't believe in atonement by blood. It doesn't come up to my ideas of what is right."

I said, "To perdition with your ideas of what is right. Do you think God is coming down here to consult you with your great intellect and wonderful brain, and find out what you think is right before he does it? " My, but you make me sick. You think that because you don't believe it that it isn't true.

I have read a great deal - not everything, mind you, for a man would go crazy if he tried to read everything - but I have read a great deal that has been written against the atonement from the infidel standpoint - Voltaire, Huxley, Spencer, Diderot, Bradlaugh, Paine, on down to Bob Ingersoll - and I have never found an argument that would stand the test of common sense and common reasoning. And if anyone tells me he has tossed on the scrap heap the plan of atonement by blood, I say, "What have you to offer that is better?" and until he can show me something that is better I'll nail my hopes to the cross.

Suffering for the Guilty

You say you don't believe in the innocent suffering for the guilty. Then I say to you, you haven't seen life as I have seen it up and down the country. The innocent suffer with the guilty, by the guilty and for the guilty. Look at that old mother waiting with trembling heart for the son she has brought into the world. And see him come staggering in and reeling and staggering to bed while his mother prays and weeps and soaks the pillow with her tears over her godless boy. Who suffers most? The mother or that godless, maudlin [drunk] bum? You have only to be the mother of a boy like that to know who suffers most. Then you won't say anything about the plan of redemption and of Jesus Christ suffering for the guilty.

Look at that young wife, waiting for the man whose name she bears, and whose face is woven in the fiber of her heart, the man she loves. She waits for him in fright and when he comes, reeking from the stench of the breaking of his marriage vows, from the arms of infamy, who suffers most? That poor, dirty, triple extract of vice and sin? You have only to be the wife of a husband like that to know whether the innocent suffers for the guilty or not. I have the sympathy of those who know right now.

This happened in Chicago in a police court. A letter was introduced as evidence for a criminal there for vagrancy. It read, "I hope you won't have to hunt long to find work. Tom is sick and baby is sick. Lucy has no shoes and we have no money for the doctor or to buy any clothes. I manage to make a little taking in washing, but we are living in one room in a basement. I hope you won't have to look long for work," and so on, just the kind of a letter a wife would write to her husband. And before it was finished men cried and policemen with hearts of adamant were crying and fled from the room. The judge wiped the tears from his eyes and said: "You see, no man lives to himself alone. If he sins others suffer. I have no alternative. I sympathize with them, as does every one of you, but I have no alternative. I must send this man to Bridewell [house of correction]." Who suffers most, that woman manicuring her nails over a washboard to keep the little brood together or that drunken bum in Bridewell getting his just deserts from his acts? You have only to be the wife of a man like that to know whether or not the innocent suffer with the guilty.

So when you don't like the plan of redemption because the innocent suffer with the guilty, I say you don't know what is going on. It's the plan of life everywhere.

From the fall of Adam and Eve till now it has always been the rule that the innocent suffer with the guilty. It's the plan of all and unless you are an idiot, an imbecile and a jackass, and gross flatterer at that, you'll see it.

Jesus' Atoning Blood

Jesus gave his life on the cross for any who will believe. We're not redeemed by silver or gold. Jesus paid for it with his blood (1 Peter 1:18). When some one tells you that your religion is a bloody religion and the Bible is a bloody book, tell them yes, Christianity is a bloody religion; the gospel is a bloody gospel; the Bible is a bloody book; the plan of redemption is bloody. It is. You take the blood of Jesus Christ out of Christianity and that book isn't worth the paper it is written on. It would be worth no more than your body with the blood taken out. Take the blood of Jesus Christ out and it would be a meaningless jargon and jumble of words.

If it weren't for the atoning blood you might as well rip the roofs off the churches and burn them down. They aren't worth anything. But as long as the blood is on the mercy seat (Lev. 16:14), the sinner can return, and by no other way. There is nothing else. It stands for the redemption. You are not redeemed by silver or gold, but by the blood of Jesus Christ. Though a man says to read good books, do good deeds, live a good life and you'll be saved, you'll be damned. That's what you will. All the books in the world won't keep you out of hell without the atoning blood of Jesus Christ. It's Jesus Christ or nothing for every sinner on God's earth.

Without it not a sinner will ever be saved. Jesus has paid for your sins with his blood. The doctrine of universal salvation is a lie. I wish every one would be saved, but they won't. You will never be saved if you reject the blood.

I remember when I was in the Y.M.C.A. in Chicago I was going down Madison Street and had just crossed Dearborn Street when I saw a newsboy with a young sparrow in his hand. I said: "Let that little bird go."

He said, "Aw, g'wan with you, you big mutt."

I said, "I'll give you a penny for it," and he answered, "Not on your tintype."

"I'll give you a nickel for it," and he answered, "Boss, I'm from Missouri; come across with the dough."

I offered it to him, but he said, "Give it to that guy there," and I gave it to the boy he indicated and took the sparrow.

I held it for a moment and then it fluttered and struggled and finally reached the window ledge in a second story across the street. And other birds fluttered around over my head and seemed to say in bird language, "Thank you, Bill."

The kid looked at me in wonder and said: "Say, boss, why didn't you chuck that nickel in the sewer?"

I told him that he was just like that bird. He was in the grip of the devil, and the devil was too strong for him just as he was too strong for the sparrow, and just as I could do with the sparrow what I wanted to, after I had paid for it, because it was mine. God paid a price for him far greater than I had for the sparrow, for he had paid it with the blood of his Son, and he wanted to set him free.

No Argument Against Sin

So, my friend, if I had paid for some property from you with a price, I could command you, and if you wouldn't give it to me I could go into court and make you yield. Why do you want to be a sinner and refuse to yield? You are withholding from God what he paid for on the cross. When you refuse you are not giving God a square deal.

I'll tell you another. It stands for God's hatred of sin. Sin is something you can't deny. You can't argue against sin. A skilful man can frame an argument against the validity of religion, but he can't frame an argument against sin. I'll tell you something that may surprise you. If I hadn't had four years of instruction in the Bible from Genesis to Revelation, before I saw Bob Ingersoll's book, and I don't want to take any credit from that big intelligent brain of his, I would be preaching infidelity instead of Christianity. Thank the Lord I saw the Bible first. I have taken his lectures and placed them by the side of the Bible, and said, "You didn't say it from your knowledge of the Bible." And I have never considered him honest, for he could not have been so wise in other things and such a fool about the plan of redemption. So I say I don't think he was entirely honest.

But you can't argue against the existence of sin, simply because it is an open fact, the word of God. You can argue against Jesus being the Son of God. You can argue about there being a heaven and a hell, but you can't argue against sin. It is in the world and men and women are blighted and mildewed by it.

Some years ago I turned a corner in Chicago and stood in front of a police station. As I stood there a patrol dashed up and three women were taken from some drunken debauch, and they were dirty and blear-eyed, and as they were taken out they started a flood of profanity that seemed to turn the very air blue. I said, "There is sin." And as I stood there up dashed another patrol and out of it they took four men, drunken and ragged and bloated, and I said, "There is sin." You can't argue against the fact of sin. It is in the world and blights men and women. But Jesus came to the world to save all who accept him.

"How Long, O God?"

It was out in the Y.M.C.A. in Chicago. "What is your name and what do you want?" I asked.

"I'm from Cork, Ireland," said he, "and my name is James O'Toole." Here is a letter of introduction." I read it and it said he was a good Christian young man and an energetic young fellow.

I said, "Well, Jim, my name is Mr. Sunday. I'll tell you where there are some good Christian boarding houses and you let me know which one you pick out." He told me afterwards that he had one on the North Side. I sent him an invitation to a meeting to be held at the Y.M.C.A., and he had it when he and some companions went bathing in Lake Michigan. He dived from the pier just as the water receded unexpectedly and he struck the bottom and broke his neck. He was taken to the morgue and the police found my letter in his clothes, and told me to come and claim it or it would be sent to a medical college. I went and they had the body on a slab, but I told them I would send a cablegram to his folks and asked them to hold it. They put it in a glass case and turned on the cold air, by which they freeze bodies by chemical processes, as they freeze ice, and said they would save it for two months, and if I wanted it longer they would stretch the rules a little and keep it three.

I was just thinking of what sorrow that cablegram would cause his old mother in Cork when they brought in the body of a woman. She would have been a fit model of Phidias [ancient Greek sculptor], she had such symmetry of form. Her fingers were manicured. She was dressed in the height of fashion and her hands were covered with jewels and as I looked at her, the water trickling down her face, I saw the mute evidence of illicit affection. I did not say lust, I did not say passion, I did not say brute instincts. I said, "Sin." Sin had caused her to throw herself from that bridge and seek repose in a suicide's grave. And as I looked, from the saloon, the fantan rooms, the gambling hells, the opium dens, the red lights, there arose one endless cry of "How long, O God, how long shall hell prevail?" (Psa. 74:10)

You can't argue against sin. It's here. Then listen to me as I try to help you.

When the Standard Oil Company was trying to refine petroleum there was a substance that they couldn't dispose of. It was a dark, black, sticky substance and they couldn't bury it, couldn't burn it because it made such a stench; they couldn't run it in the river because it killed the fish, so they offered a big reward to any chemist who would solve the problem. Chemists took it and worked long over the problem, and one day there walked into the office of John D. Rockefeller, a chemist and laid down a pure white substance which we since know as paraffine [paraffin wax].

You can be as black as that substance and yet Jesus Christ can make you white as snow. "Though your sins be as scarlet they shall be as white as snow." (Isa. 1:18)

Backsliding

"Thy own wickedness shall correct thee. Thy backsliding shall reprove thee. Know therefore and see that it is an evil thing and bitter that thou hast forsaken the Lord thy God, and that my fear is not in thee, saith the Lord God of Hosts"

Jeremiah 11:19

• • •

Many start the voyage of the Christian life under sending skies and upon smooth waters, but as they sail out of the harbor the sky becomes dark and the craft of their religion crashes upon the rocks. At first they are careful to obey the command of God, but after the revival they neglect their duties and finally come to wreck.

God speaks much of the sin of backsliding, and in the Bible has spoken of it in many places. There are all kinds of backsliding.

First, there is the careless kind. The invitation is never given at the revival but there are those who will respond to it, and for a time will live as Christians should. Then, when the revival is over and the routine of everyday life begins, they slip gradually back into their former ways. They become negligent and drift back to the old haunts and the old gang.

Oh, it is easy to think of things divine when the revival is on and there is inspiration on every side and the bands are playing and the crowds are marching.

I've sometimes thought, almost, that it might be a Godsend to many a community if it could only be swept by typhoid fever or pneumonia or scarlet fever just after a good revival and before the people have a chance to slide back.

The second class of backsliders is the class that started soberly and seriously, but not seriously enough. They do not make a complete surrender. If you secure a balloon with 100 ropes and cut 99 of them, the balloon will still be held, but don't cut the shore lines, they have failed to cut loose from sin, and it is drawing them back.

A friend of mine holding a meeting, asked how many who were present had been Christians, but were now backsliders. Finally forty fessed up. Then he asked them for the reasons for their falling away. Finally a man got up and said he backslid through believing that he could be a Christian and keep his store open on Sundays.

A young lady arose and said that she backslid because of cards. A friend had given a card party and she had to give one in reciprocity. She said she had invited a young man to attend, but that he didn't know what kind of a party it was to be. He came, but when he found out he said he was sorry, but he must go, for he could not stay there. "I admired him for his loyalty to his religion, he made me feel that I wasn't worthy to have my name as a church member," the young lady said.

Another man stood up and said: "I backslid when I voted for the saloon." You bet he did or he would not have voted for the dirty, rotten thing. Why, he backslid before he voted that ticket, or he wouldn't have voted it.

A young lady said: "I thought I could be a member of the church and dance." Sure she could. You can be a member of the church and a burglar too, but not a member of the body of Christ. She said, "I attended a dance and found my desire to pray diminishing. I attended another and I found my desire to pray had become nebulous. And then," she said, "my desire to pray disappeared."

I tell you I never saw a drinking, dancing, card playing Christian who amounted to anything. The dance is a quagmire of wreckage. It's as rotten as hell. You wait until I get at it.

I believe more people in the church backslide because of the dance, card playing and theatre gadding then through the saloons. But hold on there, don't you think for a minute that I'm in favor of the dirty, stinking, rotting saloons.

I'm against a lot of amusements popular among church members, as you people are going to find out before I am through in Boston. I don't give that (snapping his fingers) whether you like my preaching or not. Understand? It's a question of whether you are interested in decency. If you live wrong you can't die right. Emerson said: "What you are speaks so loudly that I cannot hear what you say.

This is an age of incompleteness of unfinished things. Life is full of half done things. Education is begun and abandoned. Obedience to the law of God is begun - and given up. People start in business - and fail. They attempt to learn a trade - and don't do it thoroughly. A hound once started running after a stag and after running for a while it saw a fox and turned after it. A little farther along it saw a rabbit and ran after that, and finally wound up holing a field mouse. So it is with so many who enter the Christian life. They started to hunt and compromised on a glass of booze. They enter a royal race, but compromised on a glass of beer or on some little gain through dishonesty.

Not every backslider is an apostate, but every apostate is a backslider. Peter was a backslider, but he came back and preached that sermon at Pentecost. Judas was a backslider, and what he did so preyed upon his mind that he did not want it. He went out but he never came back.

I have never tabooed but two towns in my life and one of them was a little town in Iowa, where I once held a meeting before I really became an evangelist. That town had an infidel club of 150 members. There were only two church members in the place, and there was an interrogation point after them at that. They could have started a founding asylum of their own in that community. My life was not safe there - they threw stones at me in the streets.

A storekeeper there told me he was going to sell out and leave the town for purely moral reasons, at a loss of about $8000.00. He said that he had daughters and that there wasn't a young man in the town that he would trust with them. He said that any young man in that town were to call on any of his daughters he wouldn't go upstairs to bed unless he had a Gattling gun he could train on the visitor at a moments notice. It is not only for here and now, it is not only for a time, but it is for eternity. It is one of the great things. All other things are incidents.

The leader of that God - forsaken, iniquitous gang was a man named Dickson, who ran a one - horse country grocery business in a place about as big as a boxcar. He had been a Christian - used to be a class-leader in a Methodist church. He kept a store. I used to pass the store as I went to preach, and I would see the bunch, as many as 40 sometimes, sitting around in the little store.

Whenever a new preacher came they would assemble to talk him over, and if old Dickson gave consent, they would go to church to hear him. I remember one old brush rat. He had bushy whiskers with a dirty brown streak down the middle, and he could spit 30 yards and hit a fly. I'll bet my life he could hit a post down there. He used to come in late, with one pant leg tucked in his boot, no coat or vest, no galoshes - just a rope around his paunch - the old son of perdition.

He'd sit down and turn the hose on the wall. He looked to me as if he had had only one bath in his life and that one when he was born. He came clattering down the aisle - old hair and beard twisted - looked like a cows tail. He started as a backslider, ended in apostasy, just as disease ends in death if not checked.

In business life, crises come unforeseen. Hard times come. When they do, you may be able to get away with a overdraft at the bank if the cashier knows you too well. At the bank of heaven no checks on God's mercy, when signed by God's loyal followers have ever been turned down. If you come with honest heart God will honor the appeal if your hands are red with blood.

In a campaign like this, for some little thing many men will sell out. There are men whose honor hang like meat in butcher shop, for sale for so much a pound. I thank God though, that most men are honest and most women are virtuous, and that even the minority can be made to yield when you preach the gospel right.

I ask about a man. "Has he reached the burning bush?" They answer, "Yes, and got past it." I ask, "Is he a K. of P.?" They say he is. I ask, "Has he jumped?" They say, "Yes." I don't know what it means to jump, for I am not a K. of P. I heard a couple of K. of P.'s talking, though ? they didn't leak. I suppose it has something to do with the initiation. I ask. "Is he an Odd Fellow?" "Yes" They tell me he will share his last dollar with a needy person, die for the widow or the orphan, put his head on the track ahead of the Black Diamond or allow himself to be shot to pieces before he would be false to the vows he took amid the scent of the orange blossoms.

That sounds like a good man, but there are lots of men who will be true in all these things, and false to Jesus Christ. They will go to church and partake of the communion, then will line up in front of some bar and tell smutty stories. True in business, true to lodge, true in society, true in the home, but a perjurer in the sight of God. If you are such a man you are a backslider - a backslider, sir, and a liar.

If I were to go to a man and say: "They say you're an old liar." Would he say, "Well, Bill, I suppose I am, but you mustn't put the standard too high for poor, weak humanity, and I'm only human." If I were to say to him, "They say you are an old thief and that they have to hide everything when you come around." Would he say he supposed it was true, but I mustn't set the standard too high for poor human nature? If I say, "They tell me that you are a rotten old libertine and that you have ruined many innocent girls, that you would crush a woman's virtue as quickly as a snake beneath your foot." Would he say he supposed it was true, but I mustn't set the standard too high for poor human nature?

No sir. If he were anything of a man at all he would say, "I demand, sir, that you prove your charges." But that's not what a man does when you charge him with being a backslider or to say that he is a liar. Oh, for the Presbyterian or Baptist or Episcopal backslider who stands up and talks about poor human nature - yet to say a man is a backslider is to say that he is a liar. Of, for power to come to you and show what you ought to be.

I can imagine a man being untrue in business. I can imagine him being untrue in politics. I can even - but it is difficult - imagine him being untrue to the vows made at the altar - but to be untrue to God! Be untrue to God and you will lose heaven and lose all. Be true to God and you will lose hell. I pray that God will so work upon the consciences of you backsliders who hear me that you will cry salt tears and turn and roll upon your pillows when you go home tonight and seek a dry spot that he may reproach you until you have been stung into a return to the God to whom you have been false.

A heathen woman named Panathea was famous for her great beauty, and King Cyrus wanted her for his harem. He sent his representatives to her and offered her money and jewels to come, but she repulsed them and spurned their advances. Again he sent them, this time with offers more generous and tempting; but again she sent them away with scorn. A third time she said "Nay." Then King Cyrus went in person to see her and he doubled and tripled and quadrupled the offers his men had made, but still she would not go. She told him that she was a wife, and that she was true to her husband.

He said "Panathea, where dwellest thee?"

"In the arms and on the breast of my husband." She said.

"Take her away." Said Cyrus. "She is of no use to me."

Then he put her husband in command of the charioteers and sent him into battle at the head of the troops. Panathea knew what this meant - that her husband had been sent in that he might be killed.

She waited while the battle raged and when the field was cleared she shouted his name and searched for him and finally found him wounded and dying. She knelt and clasped him in her arms, and as they kissed, his lamp of life went out forever.

King Cyrus heard of the mans death and came to the field. Panathea saw him coming, careening on his camel like a ship in a storm. She called, "Oh, husband! He comes - he shall not have me. I was true to you in life and will be true to you in death." And she drew her dead husband's poniard from its sheath, drove it into her own breast and fell dead across his body.

King Cyrus came up and dismounted. He removed his turban and knelt By the dead husband and wife and thanked his God that he had found in his kingdom one true and virtuous woman that his money could not buy nor his power intimidate.

A person of Boston, preachers, the problem of this century is the problem of the first century. We must win the world for God and we will win the world for God just as soon as we have men and woman who will be faithful to God and will not lie and will not sell out to the devil.

Broken Down Altars

"He repaired the altar of the Lord that was broken down"

I Kings 18:30

• • •

There is something more than history in the chapter from which my text is taken, just as there is always more in a picture than is seen at first glance.

The state of affairs at this time the chapter opens was as bad as is possible for the human mind to conceive. The country was in an awful condition because of idolatry, adultery and all other sins associated with a nation that had forgotten God and was given, unbridled, to all lust and evil desires.

That talk had in it no "as it were", "in a degree", "perhaps", or "in a measure" or "so to speak".

He didn't qualify it by any adjectives; every word had a ring like chilled steel as it cut like a Damascus blade into the putrefying abscesses of his day. Ahab and Jezebel were on the throne. A more vicious, iniquitous, rotten man or vile woman never disgraced the earth than these two. Wickedness had the right of way throughout the kingdom; Ahab and Jezebel set the pace and others followed. There were no depths of iniquity, adultery, licentiousness and vileness to which Ahab and Jezebel did not sink. Baal was worshiped; true religion was on the sidetrack, and hell had the main line.

It is true that there were a few faithful, like Obadiah and Naboth, who had not bowed to Baal, but they were in a sad minority. Many had been compelled to hide in caves and dens. If it was a woman who dared say she believed in and worshiped Jehovah, she was an outcast and her children were murdered;

if it was a man, he was subjected to infamies that no tongue would attempt to describe. So rampant had idolatry, adultery, and kindred evils had become that in order to try to stem the deadly tide, God sent the prophet Elijah to shut off the water supply and bring on the famine.

As we read the Bible we will notice that always in a dark time God sends a prophet to arouse, stir and call the people back to the true God.

So in this instance, when the situation looked dark, God sent His messenger to warn the people of the judgment which they were bringing on themselves because of sin and iniquity. The old Tishbite bobbed up before weak-kneed Ahab with all the abruptness of a thunderclap out of a clear sky, and without banners or bands or furbelows or salaam, spoke out in the first breath in a way that brought a deadly pallor upon the cheeks of the miserable wretch Ahab:" As the Lord of hosts liveth..." (I Kings 18:15)."As the Lord of hosts liveth, before whom I stand..." cried the prophet. that ought to be the preacher's cry ever y time he walks into the pulpit. That kind of faith makes the devil get up and dust every time! Such confidence in God as the prophet had as he stood before Him would make granite out of soapstone. And to know God as Elijah knew Him, and to have the same unbroken sense of His presence, is better preparation for a great career in the ministry than a degree from any college you can name. I am not discounting the value of education. I consider a mind without education as something like marble in a quarry, which shows none of the inherent beauty until the skill of the polisher fetches out the color and discovers every ornamental vein that runs through the marble. Education draws out many virtues and perfections which otherwise would never come to the surface and never be seen. I believe in education, but education alone cannot make character-never! It takes acquaintance with God to do that.

It takes purity of heart as well as brilliancy of intellect to make one great for God.

But I have no sympathy with anybody who would exclude anyone, educated or uneducated. "Seek ye first the kingdom of God" is as much in force tonight as it was two thousand years ago. Any man who does that will have a stirring time and will give the devil the best run for his money he ever had.

Nothing was as much needed in Israel as a sweeping revival: and God sent the right man to bring it about. Let us see how Elijah did it.

Elijah Was Sensational

He repaired the altar of the Lord that was broken down. Elijah did his work in a way that was natural but unconventional. He had backbone. He wasn't pinned down or dominated by the personality of other men. He didn't try to add anybody's peculiarities or eccentricities; he had plenty of his own and the nerve to use them, too, and to be himself.

The preacher who is afraid to be like Elijah in this respect will be as weak in his ministry as Samson with his hair cut: he will have no power. I tell you, whenever God calls a man to preach, He expects him to do it as naturally as he sneezes or snores. His individuality is to him what the steel frame is to a skyscraper.

And when he surrenders it, he becomes like other people. Down go his ministerial methods; his candlestick is taken away, and God casts him into the dust of His displeasure.

Lots of us are afraid that we do something sensational. I have no more patience with such a man than I have with a horse that will shy at a wheelbarrow, or a woman who will go into hysterics over the sight of a mouse.

Everything that Elijah did was sensational; that is why he aroused the country. If shutting off the water supply, shutting up the heavens for three years so there was not a drop of rain or dew to fall on the earth, wasn't sensational, trot out something that was. It raised the biggest stir that that whiskey-soaked, licentious, idolatrous, corrupt, godless, blasphemous country had ever seen or had ever recorded; and it made Ahab and Jezebel mad enough, I think, to spit fire.

If you wish to see a dead church awakened, do something out of the ordinary. There's plenty of Bible authority for not pushing a thing aside just because it seems sensational.

When Noah built the ark and loaded it with strange cargo, that was a sensation.

When Jonah walked down the streets of Nineveh covered with seaweed crying, "Repent! Repent!"-that was sensational. Jesus Christ created a sensation when He went into the synagogue at the beginning of His ministry and taught, not as the sribes, but as one who had authority.

Get a Little Enthusiasm for Jesus!

The preacher who can't preach as one who has authority has no call from God to open his mouth! Matthew 23 is sensational preaching in words that cut like a razor.

John the Baptist was sensational in what he said as well as in what he did, and in the clothes that he wore; and because he was not like one of the bunch, all Jerusalem and Judaea came out to hear God's lion-hearted preacher hurl anathemas of the Lord into the ranks of sin-high, low, rich and poor!

"Why don't people go to church?" is a question always asked. My guess is that it is because it is too much like going to a cemetery or a funeral parlor. Put more life in it and you won't have so many complaints. Many a time the prayer meeting is dead because a corpse is leading it. When Ahab saw Elijah, he put on a long, prayer-meeting face and with a sort of sanctimonious whine said to him, "Art thou he that troubleth Israel?"

The prophet of God came back with an uppercut and old Ahab got it under the fifth rib. Elijah straightened up like a fire ladder and, with a look that went through that old licentious king like an x-ray, thundered out, "I have not troubled Israel; but thou, and thy father's house, in that ye have forsaken the commandments of the Lord and followed Baalim." If that wasn't sensational, show me something that was! Elijah expected results from his kind of preaching. If some preachers would talk that plain to some of the big sinners on the front seats, we would soon see them begin to crowd the pews. If your churches are full of men who are working overtime for the devil-working seven days and then doing overtime at night-tell them so! If you will call a spade a spade, you will hear things begin to rattle like castanets for Jesus Christ.

One reason why there are so few revivals and why religion and morality are at such an awful low tide is because there is so little of the Tishbite kind of preaching done today to the chief sinners who occupy the chief seats in the synagogues. If Bible results are expected, there must be Bible preaching. God will honor that, no matter who may do the preaching.

I wouldn't give a rap for preaching which never lets a sinner know he is an old hell-bound sinner. There is sure to be discontent and disappointment for the preacher who is always shooting with nothing in his gun but bird shot. When David killed Goliath, he did it because he went against him with suitable ammunition. He loaded his sling according to the size of the job that he had on hand. Oh, some would have tried to kill the giant with a little sand in a blowpipe; but you can't do it that way. David didn't waste any time skirmishing for position; he took dead aim and put enough muscle behind the throw to crack the giant's bean the first throw out of the box. If he had only meant to wing him, there would have been no mourning in the camp of the Philistines. Where no definite result is expected, nothing out of the common will happen. Elijah trusted God to take care of the consequences.

The next thing we learn about Elijah is-he knew his God well enough to trust Him. Some of us are so very slightly acquainted with the Lord that we are afraid to do this. many of us get little help from God because we are afraid to trust Him to do very much for us. We won't trust Him any further than we have to. We are like the little girl who said, "I don't have to pray anymore that I won't get scarlet fever because I've got a sulfur bag around my neck." We won't go any further than we seemingly have to for the Lord.

Elijah had a God who made the ravens feed him. The widow's oil and meal failed not. He wasn't afraid of anything that could happen. So many of us are, and that is why we accomplish so little. As soon as the Lord told Elijah to go show himself to Ahab, Elijah girded his loins and started out. He didn't loose a minute considering what great odds were against him; he thought only of the help God would give him to go out and win that conflict.

Think of the help that God will give you to succeed in life, then you will not moan about the tremendous odds against you when you try to live for Jesus and His truth. Faith says; "Amen" to everything God says. Faith takes God at His word, without any "if's" or "and's". Faith says, "I believe it" and rests on that and stands pat for Jesus. If some of us had had more raven experiences yesterday, there would be more mountains moved for God today. We wouldn't go through this life as nonentities, accomplishing nothing for Jesus and His truth.

The prophet knew his God well enough to set out for the front without a tremor, and when he got there, he wasn't afraid of what would happen. His only concern was to meet the conditions as they had been made known to him, knowing that when he had done his prayerful best, he could trust God to take care of the consequences. When a farmer plows his ground and plants the seed, he has done his best; then he has to trust God to make that seed grow. When he puts that seed in the ground, he trusts the rest to a law which he cannot Understand, a law which he did not originate and which he cannot control. When you have done your prayerful best, you can bank on it that God Almighty will do His part. You never need fear or lose any sleep over the Lord. When Elijah challenged the opposition, he defied them to their worst, giving them all the rope they wanted.

Elijah Asks That They Choose Whom They will Serve; We, Too, Must Choose!

A great camp meeting, or revival was to be held on Mount Carmel. The opposition did all the advertising. Hear this:" Ahab sent unto all the children of Israel, and gathered the prophets together unto Mount Carmel. And Elijah came and said, How long halt ye between two opinions? If the Lord be God, follow him; but if Baal, then follow him." He said," Take your choice!" That is fair enough, isn't it? Nothing could be more reasonable.

If we are better by all getting drunk, them let us all quit being sober and go and get drunk.

If we are better because we curse and do not pray, let us all quit praying and go to cursing. If we are better because we are impure, then let us all stop living decent lives and go out and live for the devil. If we are better with saloons and beer joints than with churches, then let us close the churches and build more breweries and saloons.

Take your choice! If you are better, if this city is better without Jesus Christ than with Him, then I'll quit, go home and stop preaching. That is a fair deal. What was fair and reasonable then, is fair and reasonable today. "How long halt ye between two opinions? If the Lord be God, follow Him; but if Baal, then follow him." Make up your mind how it will be - the Lord God or the devil.

Now if the Bible came from God, find out what it tells you to do, then do it. If it is God's book, you have to do that or God Almighty is against you just as sure as you breathe. If the Bible comes from God, then there must be an easy way for every willing mind to find it out. If you want to know if the Bible came from God, square your life by its teachings and see if it will not make out of you the kind of man it says it will.

Give it a chance! Give it a test! The fact that God proved His existence on Mount Carmel is proof that God can do it today in Richmond. And He will do it every honest doubter who wants to know.

Elijah's Faith Held Midst Tremendous Opposition

Now the purpose of that meeting on mount Carmel was to have the people know that there was a God, and to have them get right with that God. That is the reason I sweat every drop of perspiration; that is the reason I preach with every ounce of my manhood. You haven't money enough in your bank vaults in Richmond to hire me to spend my energy and strength if I didn't believe that you were bound for Hell without Christ.

The man is either insane or a fool who deliberately fights against God and lives without God. Why, it would be as wise for him to stand on a railroad track and contest his strength with that of steel and steam as to fight against God.

It always thrills me to the end of my toes to see how bravely the old prophet of God stood up before that jeering, howling, sneering, blatant, blaspheming mob of licentious, adulterous, degenerate cutthroats who stood there and defied him. How utterly indifferent he was to the tremendous odds that were against him!

And, judging by appearances, all were against him.

It didn't look as if God were within a hundred miles of that meeting on top of mount Carmel. The whole country was reeking and stinking with filth; and as the old prophet of God stood up and scanned the blackened plains-turned black because no rain or dew had fallen on them-there wasn't a green thing in sight. As he looked into the brutal faces of that mop of blasphemers, jeering and sneering upon him, nothing but unshaken confidence in God could have kept him from stampeding and hitting it for the woods. But his faith held him!

Oh, faith is a mightier force than dynamite and electricity! Elijah helped many as he stood there alone. And if science and discovery can take the Bible from us, then the sooner they do it , the better. If the Bible came from God, you can no more hurt it by anything blatant blasphemers can say than the waves of the ocean can be stopped by blowing a tin whistle against them. If the Bible came from God, nothing you can do can hurt it, anymore than you can dam Niagara Falls with toothpicks, any more than you can knock Gibraltar down by shooting green peas against it with a popgun. And if the preacher has no faith, it becomes apparent when things go wrong. If he undertakes to hold a meeting and it rains the opening night, it chills his marrow. He is sure that it isn't God's set time to work, if those whom he counted on are sick or away from home, or if they knock him and won't come near him. How anxious he is if the janitor goes over to the side of the devil and the building is too hot or too cold. And he concludes that God has forsaken him if the organist gets on her high horse and won't come out and play, and if there is nobody present to lead the singing. Think of Elijah. In spite of all that was against him, he could stir up the opposition to do their worst. He said to them," Cry louder!" as they cried for old Baal. " Cry louder; perhaps he's asleep! Or maybe he's gone off to hunt or fish; cry louder and awaken him!"

Elijah Urged Immediate Decision

He addressed himself to the conscience of the people. That is my aim when I preach. He urged immediate decision according to their honest conviction. You do the same! If everyone would act according to his or her conviction, there wouldn't be a sinner left on God's earth.

He said," if the Lord be God, follow him"-appealing to their conscience and reason. Now he gave the people to understand that God would manifest himself in a God-like way.

In these days we are prone to belittle the work of the Holy Spirit. We depend too little on God and too much on the kitchen, or the choir loft, or something or somebody.

Miraculous work of grace must be expected and prayed for God is still the wonder-working God and He always will be. The salvation of a sinner is as much a miracle as the raising of the dead.

Human Conditions Must Be Met

God has spiritual laws that are as positive in their working and as subject to conditions as the natural laws. The laws of faith are just as certain as the laws of steam and electricity. There are laws of spiritual growth and fruitage, just as there are laws that govern the growth of a potato or a hill of corn. And to secure spiritual results, human conditions must be set.

The man who plows with a forked stick gets all the crop that he deserves. And the man who prays the same old rat-eaten prayer is on the same par with him. Get something new! To have God's help in obtaining a crop, the farmer has to do certain things, at certain times, in certain ways; if he doesn't, there will not be a potato for him to stick his fork into, nor a loaf of bread for him to cut. If one doesn't work in harmony with God, then he can have nothing to eat.

There are, I say, spiritual laws in this old world, just as there are natural laws. And to have God's help in spiritual things one must put himself in right relationship with God. The farmer must put himself in right relationship with God and in right relationship with the ground and nature by plowing and preparing it, then by planting the seed.

You must put yourself in right relationship with God or He can do you no good. You have to put yourself in right relationship with the physician by taking his medicine and following his directions; else all the skills on God's green earth will never drive the disease away.

There are natural laws to follow.

There is common sense in everything. The prophet used it when he prepared the broken-down altar. He knew it was a waste of breath to pray for God to answer by fire if he did not do his part. It is absolutely useless to ask Him to save and bless this city if the church and preacher do not do their part. Elijah was smart enough to know that.

And before you can pray right, you must begin to live right. Whatsoever is wrong must be righted. Even if it is as valuable to you as your right eye or arm, get rid of it if it is wrong, if you want God's blessing and favor and partnership with you. When this kind of repentance takes place, then the step from death to life is a mighty short one.

Rebuild Your Broken-Down Altars

He repaired the altar of sacrifice when it was broken down. Oh, God's warriors must first be God's worshipers. Uncle Sam's soldiers must first be Uncle Sam's citizens! Get things cleared away. If you want Heaven on your side, the broken-down altars must be rebuilt in your heart. Give yourself to God. Confess your sins. Stand as a solid phalanx for Christ.

There are enough men and women in this tabernacle tonight to rewrite the religious and moral history of this God-forsaken, whiskey-soaked city and transform it for Jesus Christ, if you would go out and do God's will, if you would line up absolutely as one man and woman for Jesus. But before God will pay any attention to a call for fire, Christians must get right. It is a great mistake to expect a crop without planting the seed. It is a great mistake to expect a blessing without first doing your part.

Christian, can anything more important command your attention than to give God a chance in your hear? Perhaps years ago something crept in your life and you have never had a moment of peace since. Whatsoever it was has poisoned your joy and has made serving God the hardest job in the world. Perhaps only God and you knew about it. Your friends never suspected, yet it has been there blighting and blasting. Wherever you go, that secret goes with you. You have cried and sighed to be free. But you haven't taken the course God pointed out to you. You have crucified your conscience.

Nothing will give back that peace until you build up that altar in your heart, renew that vow and covenant. Take a clean-cut stand for Jesus. Until you do, you will stay as cold and unresponsive as a stone.

Did you quarrel with someone? Did hate get a foothold? Did someone wrong you whom you think you can never forgive? Ask God to take the bitterness out, or give you grace to get rid of it. God stands pledged to help; you do not have to do it in your own strength.

No matter what has broken down the altar, build it up. Maybe it is the breaking of vows, or neglect of prayer, or neglect of family worship, or failure to get anything worthwhile done for God; maybe it is that you never go to prayer meeting, or that your business practices are crooked, or that you have been a coward about witnessing for Christ.

If you have one drop of red blood in your veins, then when a man talks about your country or your wife, you will knock him down. Yet you will stand around and let somebody damn and curse God and spew out his maledictions against the church, and never open your mouth in protest! Brother, your altar is broken down! Build it up and see what the Lord will do.

The broken-down altar at Mount Carmel was built up-not in the name of the prophet, not in the name of the scribes, but Elijah built up the broken altar in the name of the Lord. And the fire of God fell. The man who undertakes anything in His name will not have the Devil for a silent partner!

The mother who undertakes to train her child in the name of the Lord will have more anxiety about his salvation than she will about her own standing in society.

Note how carefully the broken-down altar was built up. Elijah began at the ground and cleared away the rubbish. A stone represented each tribe. He took the stones according to the twelve tribes of Israel, leaving out not one stone; if he had, there would have been no fire all that day. God is particular about important things. Now don't try to short measure God. When God says 36 inches for a yard, don't make it 32. When God says one hundred cents on a dollar, don't make it 94. When God says 2,000 pounds for a ton, 1,700 won't work. Don't try to put one over on God.

Do you remember what happened to Ananias and Sapphira when they held back part of the possessions and lied? Yes, their dead bodies were carried on out to the place of the dead. If God says 12 stones, He won't take 10. You can't get through with 11 if God says 12. Don't try to cover up the rubbish. No; clear it away if you want His blessings.

How particular the surgeon is to sterilize his instruments in order that all the dangerous germs may be kept from the wound and thus keep the patient from being put into the grave. And before fire will fall from Heaven there must be a clean place for it to fall. If the clean place is prepared, then it will come.

How is your praying? Unselfish? Or is it, "God bless me, my wife and my son John"? Are you unselfish in what you want to do? Is there anybody you won't speak to? When you get down on your knees, is there hatred in your heart against someone? Then He won't listen. The command to forgive is as positive as the command not to steal, not to commit adultery. No difference. It is just as positive as the command to insulate before you touch a wire.

Do what God says-step by step, not mile by mile. Never mind about tomorrow. We may not have a chance to do anything tomorrow; do it today and see if God doesn't bless you.

Elijah Expected Results

The next thing I notice is, Elijah went to the mountain prepared for results. He had no doubt about its being God's set time to work. He knew God so well that he was willing to meet the horde for Him. That is why he nagged the opposition to do their worst.

Trust God to give you great things. Don't be afraid of the Devil outflanking the Lord. Never! God has never lost a battle and God will never lose a battle.

Elijah wanted the prophets of Baal to humble themselves. He knew that the more fuss they made, the easier it would be to show that they were a bunch of frauds and humbugs.

It has been computed by naturalists that one mustard plant will ripen and scatter through a season thousands of seeds, and that if they all took root and grew and then scattered their seeds, in ten years all vegetation in the United States would be choked out and killed.

One saloon or beer joint in a community can smother, choke and kill enough manhood, womanhood and childhood to blight the entire community.

I read of a woman in New York called "Typhoid Mary." She was known by scientists as a carrier of the dreaded disease. After recovering from typhoid fever, a strange phenomenon happened- the germ remained with her. Wherever she went she scattered those germs. Giving typhoid fever to scores of people. To keep from further spreading the germs, she was finally put in a hospital.

The saloon is a germ-spreader, spreading the germ of drunkenness, the germ of crime, the germ of poverty, the germ of hereditary mental and physical weakness.

Liquor curses and blights the world!

Said a fellow to me the other day, "A glass of beer never hurt anybody." Of course he lied. A glass of beer never did anybody any good. It is that first glass that always leads to a drunkard's grave. If a man never took the first one, he would never take the last one.

Now nothing was slighted, and nothing was hurried through. Too many of you are in a hurry to get this meeting over. You pay closer attention to your watch than to the preacher. Men will go fishing and stand up to their knees in water for hours without even a nibble, and say they are having a good time. Yet they will fidget around when they go to church like a boy with a hornet in his pants! Don't be in a hurry with God. You can't put the pressure on when you want to get through.

Be Sure You Pray to the Right God!

In their prayer meetings, the prophets of Baal were as much in earnest as anybody else. They called on Baal from morning until evening, saying, "O Baal, hear us!" They tore their clothes, they cut themselves until blood gushed out, thinking that that self-inflicted suffering might appeal to Baal.

Elijah said, "Cry louder! You've got on the soft petal. Cry louder! He's talking or perhaps he's hunting, or he's gone on a journey, or perhaps he's asleep or gone joy-riding! Cry louder!"

Hold on! It's a waste of time to pray to the wrong god. Don't pray to money; don't pray to culture; don't pray to philanthropy; don't pray to social greatness!

Baal never heard-never! And he will never hear. Elijah addressed a prayer to the God from whom he expected help. And he had his answer before sundown! The three years that he spent out there in the cave taught him how to get a prayer through to the throne of God in three minutes-something that has never been taught in any theological seminary!

Charon and Serapis had their drawbacks, yes; but they also had their advantages. War has both its advantages and its drawbacks. Many of the blessings, which we enjoy today, were bought with blood on the battlefield. There are some things that you never get without war. Nobody wants war. But there are some things we never get without it. Never! Therefore, out in the cave Charon and Serapis had their drawbacks-as well as their advantages.

I have met a lot of people on my
Journey here below
Who were always discontented, grumbling
About their lot of woe;
Never seemed to know the blessings
that a thrill might secrete,
Or in passing take a lesson from the
Hobo on the street.
But they fancied that the roses should
Be grown without a thorn;
That it ought to rain at midnight and
Be pleasant in the morn;
They never paused to listen, nor to
Reason out alone
That luster of the jewel is due to
The grinding of the stone!

Elijah called upon the God of Abraham, Isaac and Jacob; the God who made the ravens feed him every morning and every night; the God who made the clouds obey Him; the God who made the stars witness that He was true; the God who burned Sodom and Gomorrah with fire; the God who drowned the world with a flood; the God who saved Noah; the God who said," Let there be light"; the God who shut the lions' mouths for Daniel; the God who didn't let the fire burn Shadrach, Meshach and Abednego in the furnace because they wouldn't bow down to Nebuchadnezzar and his idol of gold. The prayer that Elijah offered to God that brought fire down from Heaven was short-only sixty-three words-and it burned up and consumed everything. When the fire fell, everyone on the mount knew it was the fire of the Lord. It licked up the water; it licked up the dust; it licked up the stone; and the people fell on their faces-all except these 450 stiff-necked, uncircumcised, black-hearted, white-livered false prophets of Baal.

Oh, hear me! God has plenty of the same kind of fire up in Heaven to pour down on us! And He will give it to us and to our country just as freely as He poured it down on the altar on Mount Carmel.

When the fire fell, how soon there was purity on the mountain! Oh, let God's blessing fall and there will not be a house of ill-fame; there will not be a drunkard; a thief, a panderer, a prostitute, there will not be a stick-up nor a gunman to do the job. There will not be one blasphemer left on God's dirt. Everything that stands in the way of the Lord will be consumed.

The idolatrous prophets-all of them-had to die before dark. What happened then will always happen when God has a chance to reveal Himself. The prophets of Baal must die. When God appears on the scene, other things must go. It won't do to parole these prophets of Baal on their good behavior. They had to do what they did on Mount Carmel-put them to the sword. They had to be slain.

You will have to slay uncleanliness; you will have to slay lasciviousness; you will have to slay adultery; you will have to slay enmity; you will have to slay strive; you will have to slay jealousy; you will have to slay wrath; you will have to slay divisions; you will have to slay heresies; you will have to slay these infamous lies that men are preaching from their pulpits that lead people away from God. You will have to slay envy; you will have to slay drunkenness; you will have to slay lying; you will have to slay stealing; you will have to slay reviling. Before the fire from God comes, the prophets of Baal must die, sir!

Do you want God's blessing? Do you want it on you home? In your church? On your city? On America?

Then slay utterly! Repair the altar of the Lord that is broken down!

The Curse of Liquor!

"I tell you that the curse of God Almighty is on the saloon."

Billy Sunday

• • •

I am the sworn, eternal and uncompromising enemy of the liquor traffic. I have been, and will go on, fighting that damnable, dirty, rotten business with all the power at my command. I shall ask no quarter from that gang, and they shall get none from me.

After all is said that can be said on the liquor traffic, its influence is degrading on the individual, the family, politics and business and upon everything that you touch in this old world. For the time has long gone by when there is any ground for arguments of its ill effects. All are agreed on that point. There is just one prime reason why the saloon has not been knocked into hell, in that is the false statement "that the saloons are needed to help lighten the taxes."

It costs fifty times more for the saloon than the revenue derived from it.

I challenge you to show me where the saloon has ever helped business, education, church morals or anything we hold dear.

You listen today and if I can't peel the bark off that damnable fallacy I will pack my trunk and leave. I say that is the biggest lie ever belched out. The wholesale and retail trade in Iowa pays every year at least $500,000 in licenses. Then, if there were no drawback, it ought to reduce the taxation 25 cents per capita. If the saloon is necessary to pay the taxes, and if they pay $500,000 in taxes, it ought to reduce them 25 cents a head. But no, the whiskey business has increased taxes $1,900,000 instead of reducing them, and I defy any whisky man on God's dirt to show one town that has the saloon where the taxes are lower than where they do not have the saloon. I defy you to show me an instance.

Crime and Idiocy

Listen! Seventy-five per cent of our idiots come from intemperate parents, 80 per cent of the paupers, 82 per cent of the crime is committed by men under the influence of liquor, 90 per cent of the adult criminals are whiskey made. The Chicago Tribune kept track for 10-years and found that 53,438 murders were committed in the saloons.

Archbishop Ireland, the famous Roman Catholic of St. Paul, said of social crime "that 75 per cent is caused by drink and 80 per cent of the poverty." I go to a family and it is broken up and I say, "what caused this?" Drink! I step up to a young man on the scaffold and say, "what brought you here?" Drink! Whence all the misery and sorrow and corruption? Invariably it is drink.

Whiskey and beer are all right in their place, but their place is in hell. The saloon hasn't one leg to stand on.

Five Points, in New York, was a spot as near like hell as any spot on earth. There are five streets that run to this point, and right in the middle was an old brewery, and the streets on either side were lined with grog shops. The newspapers turned a search light on the districts, and before they could stop it the first thing they had to do was to buy the old brewery and turn it into a mission, and today it is a decent, respectable place.

Look at Kansas. It is dry. In 85 of 105 counties in Kansas there is not one idiot. In 38 counties they have not a single pauper in the poorhouse, and there are only 600 dependents in the whole State. In 65 counties in Kansas they did not have a single prisoner in the county jails in the year 1912, and in some of the counties the grand jury hasn't been called to try a criminal case in 10 years.

Sum of All Villainies

The saloon is the sum of all villainies. It is worse than war or pestilence. It is the crime of crimes. It is parent of crimes and the mother of sins. It is the appalling source of misery and crime in the land and the principal cause of crime. It is the source of three-fourths of the taxes to support that crime. And to license such an incarnate fiend of hell is the dirtiest, low-down, damnable business on top of this old earth. There is nothing to be compared to it.

The Legislature of Illinois appropriated $6,000,000 in 1908 to take care of the insane people in the state, and the whiskey business produces 75 per cent of the insane. That is what you go down in your pocket for to help support. If I remember rightly the Legislature appropriated nearly $9,000,000 to take care of the state institution. Do away with the saloon, and you will close these institutions. The saloons make them necessary, and they make the poverty and fill the jails and the penitentiaries. Who has to pay the bills? The landlord who doesn't get the rent because the money goes for whiskey; the butcher and the grocer, and the charitable person who takes pity on the children of drunkards, and the tax payer who supports the insane asylums and other institutions that the whiskey business keeps full of human wrecks.

Do away with the cursed business and you will not have to put up to support them. Who gets the money? The saloon keepers and the brewers, and the distillers, while the whiskey fills the land with misery and poverty and wretchedness and disease and death and damnation and it is being authorized by the will of the sovereign people.

Last year the corn crop was 2,553,732,000 bushels, and it was valued at $1,250,000,000. Secretary Wilson says that the breweries use less than 2 per cent; I will say that they use 2 percent. This would make 51,000,000 bushels, and at 50 cents a bushel, that would be about $25,000,000. I'll be generous with the dirty, rotten gang.

Drink and Bankruptcy

Now listen! In 1912 the income of the United States government and the cities and towns and counties from the whiskey business was $134,000,000. That is putting it liberally. You say that's a lot of money. Well, last year the working men spent $2,200,000,000 for drink, and it cost $1,200,000,000 to care for the judicial machinery. In other words, the whiskey business cost us $3,400,000,000, I will subtract from that the dirty $350,000,000 which we got, and it leaves $3,000,000,000 in favor of knocking the whiskey business out on purely a money business.

And listen! Last year we spent $600,000,000 for our paupers and criminals, insane, orphans, feeble minded, etc., in the United States, and 82 per cent of our criminals are whiskey made and 75 per cent of the paupers are whiskey made. Our national increase in wealth was only $5,000,000,000, so you can figure out how long it will take us to go into bankruptcy with that cussed business on our backs. The average factory hand earns $500 a year, and it costs us $5,200 a year to support each of our whiskey criminals. There are 335,000 enrolled criminals in the United States and 80,000 in jails and penitentiaries. Three-fourths were sent there because of drink, and then they have the audacity to say the saloon is needed for money revenue. Never was there a baser lie.

"But," says the whiskey fellow, "we would lose trade, the farmer would not come to town to trade." You lie. Say, when you put up the howl that if you didn't have the saloons the farmer won't trade-say, Mr. Whiskey Men, why do you dump money into politics and back the Legislatures into the corner and fight to the last ditch to prevent the enactment of county local option?

Scared of Farmers

You know if the farmers were given a chance they would knock the whiskey business into hell the first throw out of the box. You are afraid. You have cold feet on the proposition. You are afraid to give the farmer a chance. They are scared to death of farmers.

When the whiskey gang tries to say its business is, not falling off it lies. I've got the last annual report of the government right here. I tell you I have an inside track on that dirty gang. This report says that there were 10,741,738 less gallons of whiskey made last year than there were in 1913. It says there were 127 fewer registered distilleries in 1914 than in 1913 in our land, which means a lot when you consider there are only 743 in the United States. Also, it says there were 33 fewer breweries in 1914 than there were in 1913.

Don't put any stock in the man who gets up in Congress, says he is a temperance man in the next breathe says prohibition is a state affair. If it is a state affair why doesn't the United States government divide the $225,000,000 revenue it collected last year with the States?

Pennsylvania produced 8,800,876 gallons of beer last year, more than any other state in the union except New York. It ranked fifth in the production of whiskey producing 8,489,062 gallons. I say the temperance question is as much a national question as slavery was in the days of '61. And if the politician hasn't the manhood to stand up and defend, then somebody else will get his job in Washington before long.

Saloon vs. Government

The saloon is strong against good government. It supports the boodle aldermen, the political boss and the political machine. And all it asks for the $30 it hands out is that it be left alone. It says, "keep your hands off and let me go on with my business of making drunkards out of the countries youth, and filling the jails and the penitentiaries and the asylums and the poorhouses."

The saloon is never identified with any movement for good government, and there was never one started that the saloon didn't oppose, tooth and nail. All the slanders and lies out about me crawled out of a grog shop. The liquor gangs press bureau has got my itinerary, just as well as I have got it, and they send out there dirty; rotten, stinking lies ahead of me. Yes, and there's always a dirty, rotten, stinking newspaper or two that will print them. But don't you think that scares me a bit? I'm not afraid of the worst old scoundrel that ever dipped his pen in the inkbottle.

I tell you, gentlemen, the American home is the dearest heritage of the people, for the people, by the people, and when a man can go from home in the morning with the kisses of his wife and children on his lips, and come back at night with an empty dinner bucket to a happy home, that man is a better man, whether white of black. Whatever takes away the comforts of home - whatever degrades that man or woman - whatever invades the sanctity of the home, is the deadliest foe to the home, to church, to state and school, and the saloon is the deadliest foe to the home, the church and the state, on top of God Almighty's dirt.

And if all the combined forces of hell should assemble and conclave, and with them all the men on earth that hate and despise God and purity and virtue - if all the scum of the earth might mingle with the denizens of hell to try to think of the deadliest institutions to home, to church and state, I tell you sir the combined hellish intelligence could not conceive of or bring an institution that could touch the hem of the garment of the open licensed saloon to damn the home and the manhood, and womanhood and business and every other good thing on God's earth.

"But," you say, "we will regulate it by high license." Regulate what by high license? You might as well try to regulate a power mill in hell.

Worse Than a Thief

It is my opinion that the saloonkeeper is worse than a thief and a murderer. The ordinary thief steals only your money, but the saloonkeeper steals your honor and your character. The

ordinary murderer takes your life, but the saloonkeeper
murders your soul.

The saloon is an infidel. It has no faith in God; has no religion.
It would close every church in the land. It would hang its beer
signs on the abandoned altars. It would close every public
school. It respects the thief, and it esteems the blasphemer; it
fills the prisons and penitentiaries. It despises heaven, hates
love, and scorns virtue. It tempts the passions. Its music is the
song of a siren. Its sermons are a collection of lewd, vile stories.
It wraps a mantle about the hope of this world to come.

It is the moral clearinghouse for rot, and damnation, and
poverty, and insanity, and it wrecks homes and blights lives
today. The saloon is a liar. It promises health and causes
disease. It promises prosperity and sends adversity. It promises
happiness and sends misery.

I tell you that the curse of God Almighty is on the saloon.
Legislatures are legislating against it. Decent society is barring
it out. The fraternal brotherhoods are knocking it out. The
Masons and Odd Fellows and the knights of Pythias and the
A. O. U. W. are closing their doors to the whiskey sellers. It is
on the downgrade. It is headed for hell; and by the grace of
God, I am going to give it a push, with a whoop, for all I know
how. Listen to me; I am going to show you how we burn our
money. It costs 20 cents to make a gallon of whiskey; sold over
the counter at 10 cents a glass it will bring $4.

We dumped nearly four times the value of the national bank
stock in the United States into the whiskey hole last year, and
we didn't fill the hole up at that. What is the matter? Whenever
the day comes when every Catholic and Protestant whose
name is on a church record votes against the saloon, that day
will saloon go to hell. I charge the church as being responsible
for the saloon, for it is strong enough to do away with it. Hell
will be so full of whiskey-voting church members that their feet
will stick out the windows.

Say, hold on a bit. Have you got a silver dollar? I am going to show you how it is burned up. We have in this country 218,000 saloons, and allowing 50 feet frontage for each saloon. It makes a street from New York to Chicago, and 5,000,000 men, woman and children go daily into the saloon for drink. And marching 20 miles a day, it would take 20 days to pass this building and marching 5 abreast they would reach 500 miles. There they go; look at them!

Half Million Enter Grog Shop

On the first day of January 500,000 of the young men of our nation entered the grog shop and began a public career, hellward, and on Dec. 31 I will come back here and summon you people and ring the bell and raise the curtain and say to the saloon and breweries: "On the first day of January I gave you 500,000 of the brain and muscle of our land, and I want them back and I have come in the name of home and church and school; father, mother, sister, sweetheart: give me back what I gave you. March out."

I count, and 18,000 have lost their appetite and have become muttering, bleary-eyed drunkards, and I say: "What is that I hear, a funeral dirge?" What is that procession? A funeral procession 3,000 miles long and 600,000 hearses in the procession. One hundred and ten thousand men die drunkards in this land of the free and the home of the brave. Listen! In an hour 80 men die drunkards, 2,000 a day and 110,000 a year. One man will leap in front of a train, another will plunge into a river, another will plunge from the dock into a lake, another will throw his hands to his head and life will end. Another will cry "mother!" and his life will go out like a burnt match.

Like Hamilcar of old, who swore eternal enmity against Rome, so I propose to perpetuate the feud against liquor traffic until the white-winged dove of temperance builds her nest on the dome of the Capitol at Washington and spreads her wings of peace, sobriety and joy over our land, which I love with all my heart.

Two Uses of Dollar

I hold a silver dollar in my hand. Come on, we are going to a saloon. We will go into a saloon and spend that dollar for a quart. It takes 20 cents to make a gallon of whiskey and a dollar to buy a quart. You say to the saloonkeeper: "Give me a quart." I will show you, if you wait a minute, how she is burned up. Here I am, John, an old drunken bum with a wife and six kids (Thank God it's all a lie.) Come on, I will go down to a saloon and throw down my dollar. It costs 20 cents to make a gallon of whiskey. A nickel will buy a quart of booze. Who gets the nickel? The farmer, for corn and apples. Who gets the 95 cents? The United States government, the big distillers, the big corporations, I am John, a drunken bum and I will spend my dollar. I have worked a week and got my pay. I go into a grog shop and throw down my dollar and I get a quart of booze. Come home with me. I stagger and reel in my wife's presence and she says: "John, what did you bring home?"

"A quart."

What will a quart do? It will burn up my happiness and my home and fill my home with squalor and want. So here is the dollar. The saloonkeeper has it. Here is my quart. There you get the whiskey end of it. Here you get the workingman's end of the saloon.

But come on. I will go to a store and spend the dollar for a pair of shoes. I want them for my son, and he puts them on his feet, and with the shoes to protect his feet he goes out and earns another dollar, and my dollar becomes a silver thread in the woof and warp of happiness and joy, and the man that owns the building gets some, and the clerk that sold the shoes gets some, and the merchant, and the traveling man, and the wholesale gets some, and the factory, and the man that made the shoes, and the man that tanned the hide, and the butcher that bought the calf, and the farmer that raised the calf, and the little colored fellow that shined the shoes, and my dollar spread itself and nobody is made the worse for spending the money.

Gang Has His Money

Say, wife, the bread that ought to be in your stomach to satisfy the cravings of hunger is down yonder in the grocery store, and your husband hasn't money enough to carry it home. The meat that ought to satisfy your hunger hangs in the butcher shop. Your husband hasn't any money to buy it. The cloth for a dress is lying on the shelf in the store, but your husband hasn't the money to buy it. The whiskey gang has his money. Why didn't the United State Congress vote to let the people have a shot at the whiskey gang? I'll tell you. The whiskey gang has a Congress backed into a corner, and is squeezing the gizzard out of it so it can't even peep.

I would like to do this. I would like to see every booze fighter get on the water wagon. I would like to summon all the drunkards in America and say:

Boys, let's cut it out and spend the money for flour, meat and calico; what do you say? Say! $500,000,000 will buy all the flour in the United States.

Say, if the man that drinks the whiskey goes to hell, the man that votes for the saloon that sold the whiskey to him will go to hell. If the man that drinks the whiskey goes to hell and the man that sold the whiskey to the man that drank it goes to heaven, then the poor drunkard will have the right to stand on the brink of eternal damnation and put his arms around the pillar of justice and say, "That isn't a square deal." If you vote for the dirty business you go to hell as sure as you live, and I would like to fire the furnace while you are there.

Some fellow says, "Dry the saloon out and the buildings will be empty." Which would you rather have, empty buildings or empty jails, penitentiaries and insane asylums? You drink the stuff and what have you to say? You that vote for it and you that sell it? Look at them painted on the canvas of your recollection.

"We will make laws for you. We must have lumber for houses."

He goes up to another mill and says: "Hey, what kind of a mill are you?"

"A grist mill?"

"What do you make?"

"Flour and meal out of wheat and corn."

"Is the finished product worth more than the raw material?"

"Yes."

"Then come on. We will make laws for you. We will protect you."

He goes up to another mill and says:

"What kind of mill are you?"

"A paper mill."

"What do you make paper out of?"

"Straw and rags."

"Well, we will make laws for you. We must have paper on which to write notes and mortgages."

He goes up to another mill and says:

"Hey, what kind of a mill are you?"

"A gin mill."

"I don't like the looks nor the smell of you. A gin mill? What do you make? What kind of a mill are you?"

"A gin mill."

Growing Boy Is Raw Material

"What is your raw material?"

"The boys of America."

(Here the evangelist summoned five small boys to the platform.)

The gin mills of this country must have 2,000,000 boys or shut up shop. Say, walk down your streets; count the homes and every fifth home has to furnish a boy for a drunkard. Have you furnished yours?

"What is your raw material?"

"American boys."

"Say, saloon, gin mill, what is your finished product?"

"Blear-eyed, low down, staggering men and the scum of God's dirt, that have gone from me and taken the count."

Go to the jails, go to the insane asylums and the penitentiaries and the homes for the feeble minded. There you will find the finished product for their dirty business. I tell you, it is the worst business this side of hell; and now you know it.

They don't even give you the pure stuff. If ever there was a jubilee in hell, it was when lager beer was invented. Not 3 per cent of the beer sold is made exclusive from barley, malt, hops and yeast. Look at the breweries. What are those sidetracks for? Why, to bring in the carloads of gincose and sugar and other things they put into the stuff. Pure beer is dark in color and bitter in taste. You poor idiot, you never drank pure beer.

Not 15 per cent of the whiskey on the market is pure stuff. When it is first distilled and pure, whiskey is the color of water. It gets its color in the aging process. Legitimately, that takes from four to eight years. But now they stick a steam pipe into the stuff and "age" it in 20 hours.

What is your raw material, saloons? American boys. Say, I would not give one boy for all the distilleries and saloons this side of hell. And they have to have 2,000,000 boys every generation. And then you tell me you are a man when you will vote for an institution like that. What do you want to do, pay taxes in money or in boys?

Say, will you line up for the prohibition? Men of Boston, Massachusetts and our nation, how many of you will promise that by the help of God you will vote against it? Stand up. Let me have a look at you!

The Curse of the Saloon

"The saloon is the sum of all villainies. It is worse than war or pestilence. It is the crime of crimes. It is the parent of crimes and the mother of sins. It is the appalling source of misery and crime in the land. And to license such an incarnate fiend of hell is the dirtiest, low-down, damnable business on top of this old earth."

Billy Sunday

• • •

Here we have one of the strangest scenes in all the Gospels. Two men, possessed of devils, confront Jesus, and while the devils are crying out for Jesus to leave them, he commands the devils to come out, and the devils obey the command of Jesus. The devils ask permission to enter into a herd of swine feeding on the hillside. This is the only record we have of Jesus ever granting the petition of devils, and he did it for the salvation of men.

Then the fellows that kept the hogs went back to town and told the peanut-brained, weasel-eyed, hog-jowled, beetle-browed, bull-necked lobsters that owned the hogs, that "a long-haired fanatic from Nazareth, named Jesus, has driven the devils out of some men and the devils have gone into the hogs, and the hogs into the sea, and the sea into the hogs, and the whole bunch is dead."

And then the fat, fussy old fellows came out to see Jesus and said that he was hurting their business. A fellow says to me, "I don't think Jesus Christ did a nice thing."

You don't know what you are talking about.

Down in Nashville, Tennessee, I saw four wagons going down the street, and they were loaded with stills, and kettles, and pipes.

"What's this?" I said.

"United States revenue officers, and they have been in the moonshine district and confiscated the illicit stills, and they are taking them down to the government scrap heap."

Jesus Christ was God's revenue officer. Now the Jews were forbidden to eat pork, but Jesus Christ came and found that crowd buying and selling and dealing in pork, and confiscated the whole business, and he kept within the limits of the law when he did it. Then the fellows ran back to those who owned the hogs to tell what had befallen them and those hog-owners said to Jesus: "Take your helpers and hike. You are hurting our business." And they looked into the sea and the hogs were bottom side up, but Jesus said, "What is the matter?" And they answered," Leave our hogs and go." A fellow says it is rather a strange request for the devils to make, to ask permission to enter into hogs. I don't know, if I was a devil I would rather live in a good, decent hog than in lots of men. If you will drive the hog out you won't have to carry slop to him, so I will try to help you get rid of the hog.

And they told Jesus to leave the country. They said:

"You are hurting our business."

Interest in Manhood

"Have you no interest in manhood?"

"We have no interest in that; just take your disciples and leave, for you are hurting our business. "That is the attitude of the liquor traffic toward the Church, and State, and Government, and the preacher that has the backbone to fight the most damnable, corrupt institution that ever wriggled out of hell and fastened itself on the public.

I am a temperance Republican down to my toes. Who is the man that fights the whisky business in the South? It is the Democrats! They have driven the business from Kansas, they have driven it from Georgia, and Maine and Mississippi and North Carolina and North Dakota and Oklahoma and Tennessee and West Virginia. And they have driven it out of 1,756 counties. And it is the rock-ribbed Democratic South that is fighting the saloon. They started this fight that is sweeping like fire over the "United States. You might as well try and dam Niagara Falls with toothpicks as to stop the reform wave sweeping our land. The Democratic party of Florida has put a temperance plank in its platform and the Republican party of every state would nail that plank in their platform if they thought it would carry the election. It is simply a matter of decency and manhood, irrespective of politics. It is prosperity against poverty, sobriety against drunkenness, honesty against thieving, heaven against hell. Don't you want to see men sober? Brutal, staggering men transformed into respectable citizens? "No," said a saloonkeeper, "to hell with men. We are interested in our business, we have no interest in humanity."

After all is said that can be said upon the liquor traffic, its influence is degrading upon the individual, the family, politics and business, and upon everything that you touch in this old world. For the time has long gone by when there is any ground for arguments as to its ill effects. All are agreed on that point. There is just one prime reason why the saloon has not been knocked into hell, and that is the false statement that "the saloons are needed to help lighten the taxes." The saloon business has never paid, and it has cost fifty times more than the revenue derived from it.

Does the Saloon Help Business?

I challenge you to show me where the saloon has ever helped business, education, church, morals or anything we hold dear.

The wholesale and retail trade in Iowa pays every year at least $500,000 in licenses. Then if there were no drawback it ought to reduce the taxation twenty-five cents per capita. If the saloon is necessary to pay the taxes, and if they pay $500,000 in taxes, it ought to reduce them twenty-five cents a head. But no, the whisky business has increased taxes $1,000,000 instead of reducing them, and I defy any whisky man on God's dirt to show me one town that has the saloon where the taxes are lower than where they do not have the saloon. I defy you to show me an instance.

Listen! Seventy-five per cent of our idiots come from intemperate parents; eighty per cent of the paupers, eighty-two per cent of the crime is committed by men under the influence of liquor; ninety per cent of the adult criminals are whisky-made. The Chicago Tribune kept track for ten years and found that 53,556 murders were committed by men under the influence of liquor.

Archbishop Ireland, the famous Roman Catholic, of St. Paul, said of social crime today, that "seventy-five per cent is caused by drink, and eighty per cent of the poverty."

I go to a family and it is broken up, and I say, "What caused this?" Drink! I step up to a young man on the scaffold and say, "What brought you here?" Drink! Whence all the misery and sorrow and corruption? Invariably it is drink.

Five Points, in New York, was a spot as near like hell as any spot on earth. There are five streets that run to this point, and right in the middle was an old brewery and the streets on either side were lined with grog shops. The newspapers turned a searchlight on the district, and the first thing they had to do was to buy the old brewery and turn it into a mission.

The Parent of Crimes

The saloon is the sum of all villainies. It is worse than war or pestilence. It is the crime of crimes. It is the parent of crimes and the mother of sins. It is the appalling source of misery and crime in the land. And to license such an incarnate fiend of hell is the dirtiest, low-down, damnable business on top of this old earth. There is nothing to be compared to it.

The legislature of Illinois appropriated $6,000,000 in 1908 to take care of the insane people in the state, and the whisky business produces seventy-five per cent of the insane. That is what you go down in your pockets for to help support. Do away with the saloons and you will close these institutions. The saloons make them necessary, and they make the poverty and fill the jails and the penitentiaries. Who has to pay the bills? The landlord who doesn't get the rent because the money goes for whisky; the butcher and the grocer and the charitable person who takes pity on the children of drunkards, and the taxpayer who supports the insane asylums and other institutions, " at the whisky business keeps full of human wrecks.

Do away with the cursed business and you will not have to put up to support them. Who gets the money? The saloonkeepers and the brewers, and the distillers, while the whisky fills the land with misery, and poverty, and wretchedness, and disease, and death, and damnation, and it is being authorized by the will of the sovereign people.

You say that "people will drink anyway." Not by my vote. You say, "Men will murder their wives anyway." Not by my vote. "They will steal anyway." Not by my vote. You are the sovereign people, and what are you going to do about it?

Let me assemble before your minds the bodies of the drunken dead, who crawl away "into the jaws of death, into the mouth of hell," and then out of the valley of the shadow of the drink let me call the appertaining motherhood, and wifehood, and childhood, and let their tears rain down upon their purple faces. Do you think that would stop the curse of the liquor traffic? No! No!

In these days when the question of saloon or no saloon is at the fore in almost every community, one hears a good deal about what is called "personal liberty." These are fine, large, mouth-filling words, and they certainly do sound first rate; but when you get right down and analyze them in the light of common old horse-sense, you will discover that in their application to the present controversy they mean just about this: "Personal liberty" is for the man who, if he has the inclination and the price, can stand up at a bar and fill his hide so full of red liquor that he is transformed for the time being into an irresponsible, dangerous, evil-smelling brute. But "personal liberty" is not for his patient, long-suffering wife, who has to endure with what fortitude she may his blows and curses; nor is it for his children, who, if they escape his insane rage, are yet robbed of every known joy and privilege of childhood, and too often grow up neglected, uncared for and vicious as the result of their surroundings and the example before them. "Personal liberty" is not for the sober, industrious citizen who from the proceeds of honest toil and orderly living, has to pay, willingly or not, the tax bills which pile up as a direct result of drunkenness, disorder and poverty, the items of which are written in the records of every police court and poorhouse in the land; nor is" personal liberty " for the good woman who goes abroad in the town only at the risk of being shot down by some drink-crazed creature. This rant about "personal liberty" as an argument has no leg to stand upon.

The Economic Side

Now, in 1913 the corn crop was 2,373,000,000 bushels, and it was valued at $1,660,000,000. Secretary Wilson says that the breweries use less than two per cent; I will say that they use two per cent. That would make 47,000,000 bushels, and at seventy cents a bushel that would be about $33,000,000. How many people are there in the United States? Ninety millions. Very well, then, that is thirty-six cents per capita. Then we sold out to the whisky business for thirty-six cents apiece - the price of a dozen eggs or a pound of butter. We are the cheapest gang this side of hell if we will do that kind of business.

Now listen! Last year the income of the United States government, and the cities and towns and counties, from the whisky business was $350,000,000. That is putting it liberally.

You say that's a lot of money. Well, last year the workingmen spent $2,000,000,000 for drink, and it cost $1,200,000,000 to care for the judicial machinery. In other words, the whisky business cost us last year $3,400,000,000. I will subtract from that the dirty $350,000,000 which we got, and it leaves $3,050,000,000 in favor of knocking the whisky business out on purely a money basis. And listen, we spend $6,000,000,000 a year for our paupers and criminals insane, orphans, feeble-minded, etc., and eighty-two per cent of our criminals are whisky-made, and seventy-five per cent of the paupers are whisky-made. The average factory hand earns $450 a year, and it costs us $1,200 a year to support each of our whisky criminals. There are 326,000 enrolled criminals in the United States and 80,000 in jails and penitentiaries. Three-fourths were sent there because of drink, and then they have the audacity to say the saloon is needed for money revenue. Never was there a baser he. "But," says the whisky fellow, "we would lose trade; I heard my friend ex-Governor Hanly, of Indiana, use the following illustrations:

"Oh, but," they say, "Governor, there is another danger to the local option, because it means a loss of market to the farmer. We are consumers of large quantities of grain in the manufacture of our products. If you drive us out of business you strike down that market and it will create a money panic in this country, such as you have never seen, if you do that." I might answer it by saying that less than two per cent of the grain produced in this country is used for that purpose, but I pass that by. I want to debate the merit of the statement itself, and I think I can demonstrate in ten minutes to any thoughtful man, to any farmer, that the brewer who furnishes him a market for a bushel of corn is not his benefactor, or the benefactor of any man, from an economic standpoint. Let us see. A farmer brings to the brewer a bushel of corn. He finds a market for it. He gets fifty cents and goes his way, with the statement of the brewer ringing in his ears, that the brewer is the benefactor. But you haven't got all the factors in the problem, Mr. Brewer, and you cannot get a correct solution of a problem without all the factors in the problem. You take the farmer's bushel of corn, brewer or distiller, and you brew and distill from it four and one-half gallons of spirits. I don't know how much he dilutes them before he puts them on the market. Only the brewer, the distiller and God know. The man who drinks it doesn't, but if he doesn't dilute it at all, he puts on the market four and a half gallons of intoxicating liquor, thirty-six pints. I am not going to trace the thirty-six pints. It will take too long. But I want to trace three of them and I will give you no imaginary stories plucked from the brain of an excited orator. I will take instances from the judicial pages of the Supreme Court and the Circuit Court judges' reports in Indiana and in Illinois to make my case.

Several years ago in the city of Chicago a young man of good parents, good character, one Sunday crossed the street and entered a saloon, open against the law. He found there boon companions. There were laughter, song and jest and much drinking. After awhile, drunk, insanely drunk, his money gone, he was kicked into the street. He found his way across to his mother's home. He importuned her for money to buy more drink. She refused him. He seized from the sideboard a revolver and ran out into the street and with the expressed determination of entering the saloon and getting more drink, money or no money. His fond mother followed him into the street. She put her hand upon turn in a loving restraint. He struck it from him in anger, and then his sister came and added her entreaty in vain. And then a neighbor, whom he knew, trusted and respected, came and put his hand on him in gentleness and friendly kindness, but in an insanity of drunken rage he raised the revolver and shot his friend dead in his blood upon the street. There was a trial; he was found guilty of murder. He was sentenced to life imprisonment, and when the little mother heard the verdict - a frail little bit of a woman - she threw up her hands and fell in a swoon. In three hours she was dead.

In the streets of Freeport, Illinois, a young man of good family became involved in a controversy with a lewd woman of the town. He went in a drunken frenzy to his father's home, armed himself with a deadly weapon and set out for the city in search of the woman with whom he had quarreled. The first person he met upon the public square in the city, in the daylight, in a place where she had a right to be, was one of the most refined and cultured women of Freeport. She carried in her arms her babe, motherhood and babyhood, upon the streets of Freeport in the day time, where they had a right to be, but this young man in his drunken insanity mistook her for the woman he sought and shot her dead upon the streets with her babe in her arms. He was tried and Judge Ferand, in sentencing him to life imprisonment said: "You are the seventh man in two years to be sentenced for murder while intoxicated."

In the city of Anderson, you remember the tragedy in the Blake home. A young man came home intoxicated, demanding money of his mother. She refused it. He seized from the wood box a hatchet and killed his mother and then robbed her. You remember he fled. The officer of the law pursued him and brought him back. An indictment was read to him charging him with the murder of the mother who had given him his birth, of her who had gone down into the valley of the shadow of death to give him life, of her who had looked down into his blue eyes and thanked God for his life. And he said, "I am guilty; I did it all." And Judge McClure sentenced him to life imprisonment.

Now I have followed probably three of the thirty-six pints of the farmer's product of a bushel of corn and the three of them have struck down seven lives, the three boys who committed the murders, the three persons who were killed and the little mother who died of a broken heart. And now, I want to know, my farmer friend, if this has been a good commercial transaction for you? You sold a bushel of corn; you found a market; you got fifty cents; but a fraction of this product struck down seven lives, all of whom would have been consumers of your products for their life expectancy. And do you mean to say that is a good economic transaction to you? That disposes of the market question until it is answered; let no man argue further.

More Economics

And say, my friends, New York City's annual drink bill is $365,000,000 a year, $1,000,000 a day. Listen a minute. That is four times the annual output of gold, and six times the value of all the silver mined in the United States. And in New York there is one saloon for every thirty families. The money spent in New York by the working people for drink in ten years would buy every working man in New York a beautiful home, allowing $3,500 for house and lot. It would take fifty persons one year to count the money in $1 bills, and they would cover 10,000 acres of ground. That is what the people in New York dump into the whisky hole in one year. And then you wonder why there is poverty and crime, and that the country is not more prosperous.

The whisky gang is circulating a circular about Kansas City, Kansas. I defy you to prove a statement in it. Kansas City is a town of 100,000 population, and temperance went into effect July 1, 1905. Then they had 250 saloons, 200 gambling hells and 60 houses of ill fame. The population was largely foreign, and inquiries have come from Germany, Sweden and Norway, asking the influence of. the enforcement of the prohibitory law.

At the end of one year the president of one of the largest banks in that city, a man who protested against the enforcement of the prohibitory law on the ground that it would hurt business, found that his bank deposits had increased $1,700,000, and seventy-two per cent of the deposits were from men who had never saved a cent before, and forty-two per cent came from men who never had a dollar in the bank, but because the saloons were driven out they had a chance to save, and the people who objected on the grounds that it would injure business found an increase of 209 per cent in building operations; and, furthermore, there were three times as many more people seeking investment, and court expenses decreased $25,000 in one year.

Who pays to feed and keep the gang you have in jail? Why, you go down in your sock and pay for what the saloon has dumped in there. They don't do it. Mr. Whisky Man, why don't you go down and take a picture of wrecked and blighted homes, and of insane asylums, with gibbering idiots. Why don't you take a picture of that?

At Kansas City, Kansas, before the saloons were closed, they were getting ready to build an addition to the jail. Now the doors swing idly on the hinges and there is nobody to lock in the jails. And the commissioner of the Poor Farm says there is a wonderful falling off of old men and women coming to the Poor House, because their sons and daughters are saving their money and have quit spending it for drink. And they had to employ eighteen new school teachers for 600 boys and girls, between the ages of twelve and eighteen, that had never gone to school before because they had to help a drunken father support the family. And they have just set aside $200,000 to build a new school house, and the bonded indebtedness was reduced $245,000 in one year without the saloon revenue. And don't you know another thing: In 1906, when they had the saloon, the population, according to the directory, was 89,655. According to the census of 1907 the population was 100,835, or an increase of twelve per cent in one year, without the grogshop. In two years the bank deposits increased $3,930,000.

You say, drive out the saloon and you kill business - Ha! Ha! "Blessed are the dead that die in the Lord."

I tell you, gentlemen, the American home is the dearest heritage of the people, for the people, and by the people, and when a man can go from home in the morning with the kisses of wife and children on his lips, and come back at night with an empty dinner bucket to a happy home, that man is a better man, whether white or black. Whatever takes away the comforts of home, whatever degrades that man or woman, whatever invades the sanctity of the home, is the deadliest foe to the home, to church, to state and school, and the saloon is the deadliest foe to the home, the church and the state, on top of God Almighty's dirt. And if all the combined forces of hell should assemble in conclave, and with them all the men on earth that hate and despise God, and purity, and virtue, if all the scum of the earth could mingle with the denizens of hell to try to think of the deadliest institution to home, to church and state, I tell you, sir, the combined hellish intelligence could not conceive of or bring an institution that could touch the hem of the garment of the open licensed saloon to damn the home and manhood, and womanhood, and business and every other good thing on God's earth.

In the Island of Jamaica the rats increased so that they destroyed the crops, and they introduced a mongoose, which is a species of the coon. They have three breeding seasons a year and there are twelve to fifteen in each brood, and they are deadly enemies of the rats. The result was that the rats disappeared and there was nothing more for the mongoose to feed upon, so they attacked the snakes, and the frogs, and the lizards that fed upon the insects, with the result that the insects increased and they stripped the gardens, eating up the onions and the lettuce and then the mongoose attacked the sheep and the cats, and the puppies, and the calves and the geese. Now Jamaica is spending hundreds of thousands of dollars to get rid of the mongoose.

The American Mongoose

The American mongoose is the open licensed saloon. It eats the carpets off the floor and the clothes from off your back, your money out of the bank, and it eats up character, and it goes on until at last it leaves a stranded wreck in the home, a skeleton of what was once brightness and happiness.

There were some men playing cards on a railroad train, and one fellow pulled out a whisky flask and passed it about, and when it came to the drummer he said, "No." "What," they said, "have you got on the water wagon?" and they all laughed at him- He said, "You can laugh if you want to, but I was born with an appetite for drink, and for years I have taken from five to ten glasses per day, but I was at; home in Chicago not long ago and I have a friend who has a pawn shop there. I was in there when in came a young fellow with ashen cheeks and a wild look on his face. He came up trembling, threw down a little package and said, 'Give me ten cents.' And what do you think was in that package? It was a pair of baby shoes.

"My friend said, 'No, I cannot take them. "But, he said, 'give me a dime. I must have a drink.' "'No, take them back home, your baby will need them.' "And the poor fellow said,' My baby is dead, and I want a drink.'"

Boys, I don't blame you for the lump that comes up in your throat. There is no law, divine or human, that the saloon respects. Lincoln said, "If slavery is not wrong, nothing is wrong." I say, if the saloon, with its train of diseases, crime and misery, is not wrong, then nothing on earth is wrong. If the fight is to be won we need men - men that will fight - the Church, Catholic and Protestant, must fight it or run away, and thank God she will not run away, but fight to the last ditch.

Who works the hardest for his money, the saloon man or you?

Who has the most money Sunday morning, the saloon man or you?

The saloon comes as near being a rat hole for a wage-earner to dump his wages in as anything you can find. The only interest it pays is red eyes and foul breath, and the loss of health. You can go in with money and you come out with empty pockets. You go in with character and you come out ruined. You go in with a good position and you lose it. You lose your position m the bank, or in the cab of tile locomotive. And it pays nothing back but disease and damnation and gives an extra dividend in delirium. tremens and a free pass to hell. And then it will let you, wife be buried in the potter's field, and your children go to the asylum, and yet you walk out and say the saloon is a good institution, when it is the dirtiest thing on earth. It hasn't one leg to stand on and has nothing to commend it to a decent man, not one thing.

"But," you say, "we will regulate it by high license." Regulate what by high license? You might as well try and regulate a powder mill in hell. Do you want to pay taxes in boys, or dirty money? A man that will sell out to that dirty business I have no use for. See how absurd their arguments are. If you drink Bourbon in a saloon that pays $1,000 a year license, will it eat your stomach less than if you drink it in a saloon that pays $500 license? Is it going to have any different effect on you, whether the gang pays $500 or $1,000 license? No. It will make no difference whether you drink it over a mahogany counter or a pine counter, it will have the same effect on you; it will damn you. So there is no use talking about it.

In some insane asylums, do you know what they do? When they want to test some patient to see whether he has recovered his reason, they have a room with a faucet m in, and a cement floor, and they give the patient a mop and tell him to mop up the floor. And if he has sense enough to turn off the faucet and mop up the floor they will parole him, but should he let the faucet run, they know that he is crazy.

Well, that is what you are trying to do. You are trying to mop it up with taxes and insane asylums and jails and Keeley cures, and reformatories. The only thing to do is to shut off the source of supply.

A man was delivering a temperance address at a fair grounds and a fellow came up to him and said: "Are you the fellow that gave a talk on temperance?" "Yes."

"Well, I think that the managers did a dirty piece of business to let you give a lecture on temperance. You have hurt my business and my business is a legal one."

"You are right there," said the lecturer, "they did do a mean trick; I would complain to the officers." And he took up a premium list and said: "By the way, I see there is a premium of so much offered for the best horse and cow and butter. What business are you in?"

"I'm in the liquor business."

"Well, I don't see that they offer any premium for your business. You ought t(? go down and compel them to offer a premium for your business and they ought to offer on the list $25 for the best wrecked home, $15 for the best bloated bum that you can show, and $10 for the finest specimen of broken-hearted wife, and they ought to give $25 for the finest specimens of thieves and gamblers you can trot out. You can bring out the finest looking criminals. If you have something that is good trot it out. You ought to come in competition with the farmer, with his stock, and the fancy work, and the canned fruit."

The Saloon a Coward

As Dr. Howard said: "I tell you that the saloon is a coward. It hides itself behind stained-glass doors and opaque windows, and sneaks its customers in at a blind door, and it keeps a sentinel to guard the door from the officers of the law, and it marks its wares with false bills-of-lading, and offers to ship green goods to you and marks them with the name of wholesome articles of food so people won't know what is being sent to you. And so vile did that business get that the legislature of Indiana passed a law forbidding a saloon to ship goods without being properly labeled. And the United States Congress passed a law forbidding them to send whisky through the mails.

I tell you it strikes in the night. It fights under cover of darkness and assassinates the characters that it cannot damn, and it lies about you. It attacks defenseless womanhood and childhood. The saloon is a coward. It is a thief; it is not an ordinary court offender that steals your money, but it robs you of manhood and leaves you in rags and takes away your friends, and it robs your family It impoverishes your children and it brings insanity and suicide. It will take the shirt off your back and it will steal the coffin from a dead child and yank the last crust of bread out of the hand of the starving child; it will take the last bucket of coal out of your cellar, and the last cent out of your pocket, and will send you home bleary-eyed and staggering to your wife and children. It will steal the milk from the breast of the mother and leave her with nothing with which to feed her infant. It will take the virtue from your daughter. It is the dirtiest, most low-down, damnable business that ever crawled out of the pit of hell. It is a sneak, and a thief and a coward.

It is an infidel. It has no faith in God; has no religion. It would close every church in the land. It would hang its beer signs on the abandoned altars. It would close every public school. It respects the thief and it esteems the blasphemer; it fills the prisons and the penitentiaries. It despises heaven, hates love, scorns virtue. It tempts the passions. Its music is the song of a siren. Its sermons are a collection of lewd, vile stories. It wraps a mantle about the hope of this world and that to come. Its tables are full of the vilest literature. It is the moral clearing house for rot, and damnation, and poverty, and insanity, and it wrecks homes and blights lives today.

God's Worst Enemy

The saloon is a liar. It promises good cheer and sends sorrow. It promises health and causes disease. It promises prosperity and sends adversity. It promises happiness and sends misery. Yes, it sends the husband home with a lie on his lips to his wife; and the boy home with a lie on his lips to his mother; and it causes the employee to lie to his employer. It degrades. It is God's worst enemy and the devil's best friend. It spares neither youth nor old age. It is waiting with a dirty blanket for the baby to crawl into the world. It lies in wait for the unborn.

It cocks the highwayman's pistol. It puts the rope in the hands of the mob. It is the anarchist of the world and its dirty red flag is dyed with the blood of women and children. It sent the bullet through the body of Lincoln; it nerved the arm that sent the bullets through Garfield and William McKinley. Yes, it is a murderer. Every plot that was ever hatched against the government and law, was born and bred, and crawled out of the grog-shop to damn this country.

I tell you that the curse of God Almighty is on the saloon. Legislatures are legislating against it. Decent society is barring it out. The fraternal brotherhoods are knocking it out. The Masons and Odd Fellows, and the Knights of Pythias and the A. O. U. W. are closing their doors to the whisky sellers. They don't want you wriggling your carcass in their lodges. Yes, sir, I tell you, the curse of God is on it. It is on the down grade. It is headed for hell, and, by the grace of God, I am going to give it a push, with a whoop, for all I know how. Listen to me. I am going to show you how we burn up our money. It costs twenty cents to make a gallon of whisky; sold over the counter at ten cents a glass, it will bring four dollars.

"But," said the saloonkeeper, "Bill, you must figure on the strychnine and the cochineal, arid other stuff they put in it, and it will bring nearer eight dollars."

Yes; it increases the heart beat thirty times more in a minute, when you consider the licorice and potash and logwood and other poisons that are put in. I believe one cause for the unprecedented increase of crime is due to the poison put in the stuff nowadays to make it go as far as they can.

I am indebted to my friend, George B. Stuart, for some of the following points:

I will show you how your money is burned up. It costs twenty cents to make a gallon of whisky, sold over the counter at ten cents a glass, which brings four dollars. Listen, where does it go? Who gets the twenty cents? The farmer for his corn or rye. Who gets the rest? The United States government for collecting revenue, and the big corporations, and part is used to pave our streets and pay our > police. I'll show you. I'm going to show you how it is burned up, and you don't need half sense to catch on, and if you don't understand just keep still and nobody will know the difference.

I say, "Hey, Colonel Politics, what is the matter with the country?"

He swells up like a poisoned pup and says to me, "Bill, why the silver bugbear. That's what is the matter with the country."

The total value of the silver produced in this country in 1912 was $39,000,000. Hear me! In 1912 the total value of the gold produced in this country was $93,000,000, and we dumped thirty-six times that much in the whisky hole and didn't fill it. What is the matter? The total value of all the gold and silver produced in 1912 was $132,000,000, and we dumped twenty-five times that amount in the whisky hole and didn't fill it.

What is the matter with the country, Colonel Politics? He swells up and says, "Mr. Sunday, Standpatism, sir."

I say, "You are an old windbag."

"Oh," says another, "revision of the tariff." Another man says, "Free trade; open the doors at the ports and let them pour the products in and we will put the trusts on the sidetrack."

Say, you come with me to every port of entry. Listen! In 1912 the total value of all the imports was $1,812,000,000, and we dumped that much m the whisky hole in twelve months and did not fill it.

"Oh," says a man, "let us court South America and Europe to sell our products. That's what is the matter; we are not exporting enough."

Last year the total value of all the exports was $2,362,000,000, and we dumped that amount in the whisky hole in one year and didn't fill it.

One time I was down in Washington and went to the United States treasury and said: "I wish you would let me go where you don't let the general public." And they took us around on the inside and we walked into a room about twenty feet long and fifteen feet wide and as many feet high, and I said, "What is this?"

"This is the vault that contains all of the national bank stock in the United States."

I said, "How much is here?"

They said, "$578,000,000."

And we dumped nearly four times the value of the national bank stock in the United States into the whisky hole last year, and we didn't fill the hole up at that. What is the matter? Say, whenever the day comes that all the Catholic and Protestant churches, just when the day comes when you will say to the whisky business: "You go to hell," that day the whisky business will go to hell. But you sit there, you old whisky-voting elder and deacon and vestryman, and you wouldn't strike your hands together on the proposition. It would stamp you an old hypocrite and you know it.

Say, hold on a bit. Have you got a silver dollar? I am going to show you how it is burned up. We have in this country 250,000 saloons, and allowing fifty feet frontage for each saloon it makes a street from New York to Chicago, and 5,000,000 men, women and children go daily into the saloon for drink. And marching twenty miles a day it would take thirty days to pass this building, and marching five abreast they would reach 590 miles. There they go; look at them!

On the first day of January, 500,000 of the young men of our nation entered the grog-shop and began a public career hellward, and on the 31st of December I will come back here and summon you people, and ring the bell and raise the curtain and say to the saloon and breweries: "On the first day of January, I gave you 500,000 of the brain and muscle of our land, and I want them back and have come in the name of the home and church and school; father mother, sister, sweetheart; give me back what I gave you. March out."

I count, and 165,000 have lost their appetites and have become muttering, bleary-eyed drunkards, wallowing in their own excrement, and I say, "What is it I hear, a funeral dirge?" What is that procession? A funeral procession 3,000 miles long and 110,000 hearses in the procession. One hundred and ten thousand men die drunkards in the land of the free and home of the brave. Listen! In an hour twelve men die drunkards, 300 a day and 110,000 a year. One man will leap in front of a train, another will plunge from the dock into a lake, another will throw his hands to his head and life will end. Another will cry, "Mother," and his life will go out like a burnt match.

I stand in front of the jails and count the whisky criminals. They say, "Yes, Bill, I fired the bullet." "Yes, I backed my wife into the corner and beat her life out. I am waiting for the scaffold; I am waiting." "I am waiting," says another, "to slip into hell." On, on, it goes. Say, let me summon the wifehood, and the motherhood, and the childhood and see the tears rain down the upturned faces. People, tears are too weak for that hellish business. Tears are only salty backwater that well up at the bidding of an occult power, and I will tell you there are 865,000 whisky orphan children in the United States, enough in the world to belt the globe three times around, punctured at every fifth point by a drunkard's widow.

Like Hamilcar of old, who swore young Hannibal to eternal enmity against Rome, so I propose to perpetuate this feud against the liquor traffic until the white-winged dove of temperance builds her nest on the dome of the capitol of 'Washington and spreads her wings of peace, sobriety and joy over our land which I love with ail my heart.

What Will a Dollar Buy?

I hold a silver dollar in my hand. Come on, we are going to a saloon. We will go into a saloon and spend that dollar for a quart. It takes twenty cents to make a gallon of whisky and a dollar will buy a quart. You say to the saloonkeeper, "Give me a quart." I will show you, if you wait a minute, how she is burned up. Here I am John, an old drunken bum, with a wife and six kids. (Thank God, it's all a lie.) Come on, I will go down to a saloon and throw down my dollar. It costs twenty cents to make a gallon of whisky. A nickel will make a quart. My dollar will buy a quart of booze. Who gets the nickel? The farmer, for corn and apples. Who gets the ninety-five cents? The United States government, the big distillers, the big corporations. I am John, a drunken bum, and I will spend my dollar. I have worked a week and got my pay. I go into a grog-shop and throw down my dollar. The saloonkeeper gets my dollar and I get a quart of booze. Come home with me. I stagger, and reel, and spew in my 'wife's presence, and she says:

"Hello, John, what did you bring home?"

"A quart."

What will a quart do? It will burn up my happiness and my home and fill my home with squalor and want. So there is the dollar. The saloonkeeper has it. Here is my quart. There you get the whisky end, of it. Here you get the workingman's end of the saloon.

But come on; I will go to a store and spend the dollar for a pair of shoes. I want them for my son, and he puts them on his feet, and with the shoes to protect his feet he goes out and earns another dollar, and my dollar becomes a silver thread in the woof and warp of happiness and joy, and the man that owns the building gets some, and the clerk that sold the shoes gets some, and the merchant, and the traveling man, and the wholesale house gets some, and the factory, and the man that made the shoes, and the man that tanned the hide, and the butcher that bought the calf, and the little colored fellow that shined the shoes, and my dollar spread itself and nobody is made worse for spending the money.

I join the Booster Club for business and prosperity. A man said, "I will tell you what is the matter with the country: it's overproduction." You lie, it is under consumption.

Say, wife, the bread that ought to be in your stomach to satisfy the cravings of hunger is down yonder in the grocery store, and your husband hasn't money enough to carry it home. The meat that ought to satisfy your hunger hangs in the butcher shop.

Your husband hasn't any money to buy it. The cloth for a dress is lying on the shelf in the store, but your husband hasn't the money to buy it. The whisky gang has his money.

What is the matter with our country? I would like to do this. I would like to see every booze-fighter get on the water wagon. I would like to summon all the drunkards in America and say: "Boys, let's cut her out and spend the money for flour, meat and calico; what do you say?" Say I $500,000,000 will buy all the flour in the United States; $500,000,000 will buy all the beef cattle, and $500,000,000 will buy all the cotton at $50 a bale. But we dumped more money than that in the whisky hole last year, and we didn't fill it. Come on; I'm going to line up the drunkards. Everybody fall in. Come on, ready, forward, march. Right, left, here I come with all the drunkards. We will line up in front of a butcher shop. The butcher says, "What do you want, a piece of neck?"

"No; how much do I owe you?" "Three dollars." "Here's your dough. Now give me a porterhouse steak and a sirloin roast."

"Where did you get all that money?"

"Went to hear Bill and climbed on the water wagon." "Hello! What do you want?" "Beefsteak."

"What do you want?" "Beefsteak."

We empty the shop and the butcher runs to the telephone. "Hey, Central, give me the slaughter house. Have you got any beef, any pork, any mutton?"

They strip the slaughter house, and then telephone to Swift, and Armour, and Nelson Morris, and Cudahy, to send down trainloads of beefsteaks.

"The whole bunch has got on the water wagon."

And Swift and the other big packers in Chicago say to their salesmen: "Buy beef, pork and mutton."

The farmer sees the price of cattle and sheep jump up to three times their value. Let me take the money you dump into the whisky hole and buy beefsteaks with it. I will show what is the matter with America. I think the liquor business is the dirtiest, rottenest business this side of hell.

Come on, are you ready? Fall in! We line up in front of a grocery store.

"What do you want?"

"Why, I want flour. What do you want? Flour."

"What do you want?"

"Flour."

"Pillsbury, Minneapolis, 'Sleepy Eye'?"

"Yes, ship in trainloads of flour; send on fast mail schedule, with an engine in front, one behind and a Mogul in the middle."

"What's the matter?"

"Why, the workingmen have stopped spending their money for booze and have begun to buy flour."

They tell their men to buy wheat and the farmers see the price jump to over $2 per bushel. What's the matter with the country? Why, the whisky gang has your money and you have an empty stomach, and yet you will walk up and vote for the dirty booze.

Come on, cut out the booze, boys. Get on the water wagon; get on for the sake of your wife and babies, and hit the booze a blow.

Come on, ready, forward, march! Eight, left, halt! We are in front of a dry goods store.

"What do you want?"

"Calico."

"What do you want?"

"Calico."

"What do you want?"

"Calico."

"Calico; all right, come on." The stores are stripped. Marshall Field, Carson, Pirie, Scott & Co., J. V. Farreu, send down calico. The whole bunch has voted out the saloons and we have such a demand for calico we don't know what to do. And the big stores telegraph to Fall River to ship calico, and the factories telegraph to buy cotton, and they tell their salesmen to buy cotton, and the cotton plantation man sees cotton jump up to $150 a bale. What is the matter? Your children are going naked and the whisky gang has got your money. That's what's the matter with you. Don't listen to those old whisky-soaked politicians who say "stand pat on the saloon."

Come with me. Now, remember, we have the whole bunch of booze fighters on the water wagon, and I'm going home now. Over there I was John, the drunken bum, The whisky gang got my dollar and I got the quart. Over here I am John on the water wagon. The merchant got my dollar and I have his meat, flour and calico, and I'm going home now. "Be it ever so humble, there's no place like home without booze."

"Two porterhouse steaks, Sally."

"What's that bundle, Pa?"

"Clothes to make you a new dress, Sis. Your mother has fixed your old one so often, it looks like a crazy quilt."

"And what have you there?"

"That's a pair of shoes for you, Tom; and here is some cloth to make you a pair of pants. Your mother has patched the old ones so often, they look like the map of United States."

What's the matter with the country? We have been dumping into the whisky hole the money that ought to have been spent for flour, beef and calico, and we haven't the hole filled up yet.

A man comes along and says: "Are you a drunkard?"

"Yes, I'm a drunkard."

"Where are you going?"

"I am going to hell."

"Why?'

"Because the Good Book says: 'No drunkard shall inherit the kingdom of God,' so I am going to hell."

Another man comes along and I say: "Are you a church member?"

"Yes, I am a church member."

"Where are you going?"

"I am going to heaven."

"Did you vote for the saloon?"

"Yes."

"Then you shall go to hell."

Say, if the man that drinks the whisky goes to hell, the man that votes for the saloon that sold the whisky to him will go to hell. If the man that drinks the whisky goes to hell, and the man that sold the whisky to the men that drank it, goes to heaven, then the poor drunkard will have the right to stand on the brink of eternal damnation and put his arms around the pillar of justice, shake his fist in the face of the Almighty and say, "Unjust! Unjust!" If you vote for the dirty business you ought to go to hell as sure as you live, and I would like to fire the furnace while you are there. Some fellow says, "Drive the saloon out and the buildings will be empty." Which would you rather have, empty buildings or empty jails, penitentiaries and insane asylums? You drink the stuff and what have you to say? You that vote for it, and you that sell it? Look at them painted on the canvas of your recollection.

The Gin Mill

"Hello, there, what kind of a mill are you?"

"A sawmill."

"And what do you make?"

"We make boards out of logs."

"Is the finished product worth more than the raw material?"

"Yes."

"We will make laws for you. We must have lumber for houses."

He goes up to another mill and says:

"Hey, what kind of a mill are you?"

"A grist mill."

"What do you make?"

"Flour and meal out of wheat and corn."

"Is the finished product worth more than the raw material?"

"Yes."

"Then come on. We will make laws for you. We will protect you."

He goes up to another mill and says:

"What kind of a mill are you?" "A paper mill." "What do you make paper out of?" "Straw and rags."

"Well, we will make laws for you. We must have paper on which to write notes and mortgages."

He goes up to another mill and says:

"Hey, what land of a mill are you?"

"A gin mill."

"I don't like the looks nor the smell of you. A gin mill; what do you make? What kind of a mill are you?"

"A gin mill."

"What is your raw material?"

"The boys of America."

The gin mills of this country must have 2,000,000 boys or shut up shop. Say, walk down your streets, count the homes and every fifth home has to furnish a boy for a drunkard. Have you furnished yours? No. Then I have to furnish two to make up.

"What is your raw material?"

"American boys."

"Then I will pick up the boys and give them to you."

A man says, "Hold on, not that boy, he is mine."

Then I will say to you what a saloonkeeper said to me when I protested, "I am not interested in boys; to hell with your boys."

"Say, saloon gin mill, what is your finished product?"

"Bleary-eyed, low-down, staggering men and the scum of God's dirt."

Go to the jails, go to the insane asylums and the penitentiaries, and the homes for feeble-minded. There you will find the finished product for their dirty business. I tell you it is the worst business this side of hell, and you know it.

Listen! Here is an extract from the Saturday Evening Post of November 9, 1907, taken from a paper read by a brewer. You will say that a man didn't say it: "It appears from these facts that the success of our business lies in the creation of appetite among the boys. Men who have formed the habit scarcely ever reform, but they, like others, will die, and unless there are recruits made to take their places, our coffers will be empty, and I recommend to you that money spent in the creation of appetite will return in dollars to your tills after the habit is formed."

What is your raw material, saloons? American boys. Say, I would not give one boy for all the distilleries and saloons this side of hell. And they have to have 2,000,000 boys every generation. And then you tell me you are a man when you will vote for an institution like that. What do you want to do, pay taxes in money or in boys?

I feel like an old fellow in Tennessee who made his living by catching rattlesnakes. He caught one with fourteen rattles and put it in a box with a glass top. One day when he was sawing wood his little five-year old boy;

Jim, took the lid off and the rattler wriggled out and struck him in the cheek. He ran to his father and said, "The rattler has bit me." The father ran and chopped the rattler to pieces, and with his jackknife he cut a chunk from the boy's cheek and then sucked and sucked at the wound to draw out the poison. -He looked at little Jim, watched the pupils of his eyes dilate and watched him swell to three times his normal size, watched his lips become parched and cracked, and eyes roll, and little Jim gasped and died.

The father took him in his arms, carried him over by the side of the rattler, got on his knees and said, "0 God, I would not give little Jim for all [the rattlers that ever crawled over the Blue Ridge mountains."

And I would not give one boy for every dirty dollar you get from the hell-soaked liquor business or from every brewery and distillery this side of hell.

In a Northwest city a preacher sat at his breakfast table one Sunday morning. The doorbell rang; he answered it; and there stood a little boy, twelve years of age. He was on crutches, right leg off at the knee, shivering, and he said, "Please, sir, will you come up to the jail and talk and pray with papa? He murdered mamma. Papa was good and kind, but whisky did it, and I have to support my three little sisters. I sell newspapers and black boots. Will you go up and talk and pray with papa? And will you come home and be with us when they bring him back? The governor says we can have his body after they hang him."

The preacher hurried to the jail and talked and prayed with the man. He had no knowledge of what he had done. He said, "I don't blame the law, but it breaks my heart to think that my children must be left in a cold and heartless world. Oh, sir, whisky did it."

The preacher was at the little hut when up drove the undertaker's wagon and they carried out the pine coffin. They led the little boy up to the coffin, he leaned over and kissed his father and sobbed, and said to his sister, "Come on, sister, kiss papa's cheeks before they grow cold." And the little hungry, ragged, whisky orphans hurried to the coffin, shrieking in agony. Police, whose hearts were adamant, buried their faces in their hands and rushed from the house, and the preacher fell on his knees and lifted his clenched fist and tear-stained face and took an oath before God, and before the whisky orphans, that he would fight the cursed business until the undertaker carried him out in a coffin.

A Chance for Manhood

You men have a chance to show your manhood. Then in the name of your pure mother, in the name of your manhood, in the name of your wife and the poor innocent children that climb up on your lap and put their arms around your neck, in the name of all that is good and noble, fight the curse. Shall you men, who hold in your hands the ballot, and in that ballot held the destiny of womanhood and childhood and manhood, shall you, the sovereign power, refuse to rally in the name of the defenseless men and women and native land? No.

I want every man to say, "God, you can count on me to protect my wife, my home, my mother and my children and the manhood of America."

By the mercy of God, which has given to you the unshaken and unshakable confidence of her you love, I beseech you, make a fight for the women who wait until the saloons spew out their husbands and their sons, and send them home maudlin, brutish, devilish, stinking, blear-eyed, bloated-faced drunkards.

You say you can't prohibit men from drinking. Why, if Jesus Christ were here today some of you would keep on in sin just the same. But the law can be enforced against whisky just the same as it can be enforced against anything else, if you have honest officials to enforce it. Of course it doesn't prohibit. There isn't a law on the books of the state that prohibits. We have laws against murder. Do they prohibit? We have laws against burglary. Do they prohibit? We have laws against arson, rape, but they do not prohibit. Would you introduce a bill to repeal all the laws that do not prohibit? Any law will prohibit to a certain extent if honest officials enforce it. But no law will absolutely prohibit. We can make a law against liquor prohibit as much as any law prohibits.

Or would you introduce a bill saying, if you pay $1,000 a year you can kill any one you don't like; or by paying $500 a year you can attack any girl you want to; or by paying $100 a year you can steal anything that suits you? That's what you do with the dirtiest, rottenest gang this side of hell. You say for so much a year you can have a license to make staggering, reeling, drunken sots, murderers and thieves and vagabonds. You say, "Bill, you're too hard on the whisky." I don't agree. Not on your life. There was a fellow going along the pike and a farmer's dog ran snapping at him. He tried to drive it back with a pitchfork he carried, and failing to do so he pinned it to the ground with the prongs. Out came the farmer: "Hey, why don't you use the other end of that fork?" He answered "Why didn't the dog come at me with the other end?"

Personal Liberty

Personal liberty is not personal license. I dare not exercise personal liberty if it infringes on the liberty of others. Our forefathers did not fight and die for personal license but for personal liberty bounded by laws. Personal liberty is the liberty of a murderer, a burglar, a seducer, or a wolf that wants to remain in a sheep fold, or the weasel in a hen roost. You have no right to vote for an institution that is going to drag your sons and daughters to hell.

If you were the only persons in this city you would have a perfect right to drive your horse down the street at breakneck speed; you would have a right to make a race track out of the streets for your auto; you could build a slaughter house in the public square; you could build a glue factory in the public square. But when the population increases from one to 600,000 you can't do it. You say, "Why can't I run my auto? I own it. Why can't I run my horse? I own it. Why can't I build the slaughter house? I own the lot." Yes, but there are 600,000 people here now and other people have rights.

So law stands between you and personal liberty, you miserable dog. You can't build a slaughter house in your front yard, because the law says you can't. As long as I am standing here on this platform I have personal liberty. I can swing my arms at will. But the minute any one else steps on the platform my personal liberty ceases. It stops just one inch from the other fellow's nose.

When you come staggering home, cussing right and left and spewing and spitting, your wife suffers, your children suffer. Don't think that you are the only one that suffers. A man that goes to the penitentiary makes his wife and children suffer just as much as he does. You're placing a shame on your wife and children. If you're a dirty, low-down, filthy, drunken, whisky-soaked bum you'll affect all with whom you come in contact. If you're a God-fearing man you will influence all with whom you come in contact. You can't live by yourself with my business?"

If I heard a man beating his wife and heard her shrieks and the children's cries and my wife would tell me to go and see what was the matter, and I went in and found a great big, broad-shouldered, whisky-soaked, hog-jowled, weasel-eyed brute dragging a little woman around by the hair, and two children in the corner unconscious from his kicks and the others yelling in abject terror, and he said, "What are you coming in to interfere with my personal liberty for? Isn't this my wife, didn't I pay for the license to wed her?" You ought, or you're a bigamist. "Aren't these my children; didn't I pay the doctor to bring them into the world?" You ought to, or you're a thief. "If I want to beat them, what is that your business, aren't they mine?" Would I apologize? Never! I'd knock seven kinds of pork out of that old hog.

The Moderate Drinker

I remember when I was secretary of the Y. M. C. A. in Chicago, I had the saloon route. I had to go around and give tickets inviting men to come to the Y. M. C. A. services. And one day I was told to count the men going into a certain saloon. Not the ones already in, but just those going in. In sixty-two minutes I could count just 1,004 men going in there. I went in then and met a fellow who used to be my side-kicker out in Iowa, and he threw down a mint julep while I stood there, and I asked him what he was doing.

"Oh, just come down to the theater," he said, "and came over for a drink between acts."

I said to my friend, "George, do you see that old drunken bum, down and out? There was a time when he was just like you. No drunkard ever intended to be a drunkard. Every drunkard intended to be a moderate drinker."

"Oh, you're unduly excited over my welfare," he said. "I never expect to get that far."

"Neither did that bum," I answered. I was standing on another corner less than eight months afterward and I saw a bum coming along with head down, his eyes bloodshot, his face bloated, and he panhandled me for a flapjack before I recognized him. It was George. He had lost his job and was on the toboggan slide hitting it for hell. I say if sin weren't so deceitful it wouldn't be so attractive. Every added drink makes it harder.

Some just live for booze. Some say, "I need it. It keeps me warm in winter." Another says, "It keeps me cool in summer." Well, if it keeps you warm in winter and cool in summer, why is it that out of those who freeze to death and are sun-struck the greater part of them are booze-hoisters? Every one takes it for the alcohol there is in it. Take that out and you would as soon drink dish water.

I can buy a can of good beef extract and dip the point of my knife in the can and get more nourishment on the point of that knife than in 800 gallons of the best beer. If the brewers of this land today were making their beer in Germany, ninety per cent of them would be in jail. The extract on the point of the knife represents one and three-quarter pounds of good beefsteak.

Just think, you have to make a swill barrel out of your bellies and a sewer if you want to get that much nourishment out of beer and run 800 gallons through. Oh, go ahead, if you want to, but I'll try to help you just the same.

Every man has blood corpuscles and their object is to take the impurities out of your system. Perspiration is for the same thing. Every time you work or I preach the impurities come out. Every time you sweat there is a destroying power going on inside. The blood goes through the heart every seventeen seconds. Oh, we have a marvelous system. In some spots there are 4,000 pores to the square inch and a grain of sand will cover 150 of them. I can strip you and cover you with shellac and you'll be dead in forty-eight hours. Oh, we are fearfully and wonderfully made.

Alcohol knocks the blood corpuscles out of business so that it takes eight to ten to do what one ought to do. There's a man who drinks. Here's a fellow who drives a beer wagon. Look how pussy he is. He's full of rotten tissue. He says he's healthy. Smell his breath. You punch your finger in that healthy flesh he talks about and the dent will be there a half an hour afterwards. You look like you don't believe it. Try it when you go to bed tonight. Pneumonia has a first mortgage on a booze-hoister.

Take a fellow with good, healthy muscles, and you punch them and they bound out like a rubber band. The first thing about a crushed strawberry stomach is a crushed strawberry nose. Nature lets the public on the outside know what is going on inside. If I could just take the stomach of a moderate drinker and turn it wrong side out for you, it would be all the temperance lecture you would need. You knew what alcohol does to the white of an egg. It will cook it in a few minutes. Well, alcohol does the same thing to the nerves as to the white of an egg. That's why some men can't walk. They stagger because their nerves are partly paralyzed.

The liver is the largest organ of the body. It takes all of the blood in the body and purifies it and takes out the poisons and passes them on to the gall and from there they go to the intestines and act as oil does on machinery. When a man drinks the liver becomes covered with hob nails, and then refuses to do the work, and the poisons stay in the blood. Then the victim begins to turn yellow. He has the jaundice. The kidneys take what is left and purify that. The booze that a man drinks turns them hard.

That's what booze is doing for you. Isn't it tune you went red hot after the enemy? I'm trying to help you. I'm trying to put a carpet on your floor, pull the pillows out of the window, give you and your children and wife good clothes. I'm trying to get you to save your money instead of buying a machine for the saloonkeeper while you have to foot it.

By the grace of God I have strength enough to pass the open saloon, but some of you can't, so I owe it to you to help you.

I've stood for more sneers and scoffs and insults and had my life threatened from one end of the land to the other by this God-forsaken gang of thugs and cutthroats because I have come out uncompromisingly against them. I've taken more dirty, vile insults from this low-down bunch than from any one on earth, but there is no one that will reach down lower, or reach higher up or wider, to help you out of the pits of drunkenness than I.

Gethsemane

"And being more in agony, He prayed more earnestly; and His sweat was as it were great drops of blood falling down to the ground."

Luke 22:24

• • •

Infidels have seized upon certain verses of Scripture and have given as reasons for their unbelief that the statement therein contained did not agree with their opinion. One of these verses is the one that I have just read - "and being in great agony, He prayed more earnestly; and His sweat was as it were great drops of blood falling down to the ground."

For, says the infidel, it is a physical impossibility for men to sweat blood. This is a lot of nonsense. Because you have two good eyes, and have always known good sight, should you say there are no blind? They have never heard of such a thing happening, they say. All right; but because you say that man has never sweat blood, don't say that God didn't.

When I was a boy I used to hear men say that the Bible couldn't be true, for it was absolutely impossible for a man to fast for forty days and live. They thought that settled it. Then along came Doctor Tanner, and he fasted for forty days. That was the first time. He fasted again for forty-six days, and he fasted a third time for sixty-two days, and after that we didn't hear any more about a fast of forty days being impossible. The infidels quit quoting Tom Paine's "Age of Reason" on that point.

When a man gets chesty and puts his old theories up against God, then God always brings a man forward to show that he is an old marplot and an old liar.

Doctor Witheroy, pastor of a Presbyterian church in Chicago - he went there from Boston - says he knew of a man who had a wayward son. He hadn't heard from that boy for nine years. Then, one day, they sent him word that his son was in prison. He had committed a murder, and he had been tried and convicted and was about to be executed. He had refused to tell anything about his family until he was face to face with death; then he told them and they wrote to the father to ask him what should be done with the body.

Doctor Witheroy said that in his agony that father sweat drops of blood. If an earthly father sweat drops of blood for one son who has just gone wrong, is it strange that Jesus should sweat drops of blood for all men when they were in danger of hell?

When Jesus sweat drops of blood there in the garden, it was a new sight for the angels. They had seen their brother angels rebel against God, and they had seen the conflict which followed and they had seen these rebel angels hurled over the battlements of Heaven. They had seen Sennacherib come up with his men, and they had seen 180,000 Assyrians laid low by the sword when the angel of God smote them in the night. They had seen Shadrach, Meshach and Abednego cast into a fiery furnace for refusing to bow themselves down to idols, and had seen them come out from it unharmed. They had seen the brave Daniel hurled into the lion's den for refusing to bow the knee to anyone save Jehovah, and they had seen him come out from the den of wild beasts alive. But never before had the angels beheld such a sight as when they looked down upon the garden of Gethsemane and saw the son of God kneeling there, sweating drops of blood as He agonized over man.

In this text there are many lessons valuable to us, and especially valuable just at this stage of the campaign.

The first lesson is that the Divine cup is bitter. It is bitter to fallen angels and fallen man, and it was bitter to the fallen Christ. Think of the sight. Think of Jesus, staining his garments with the bloody sweat, not because of any sin or fault of his own, for He was without sin, but because of His anguish over man.

God hates sin and so do I, so will every man on this earth who lays any claim to decency. If you don't hate sin you will if you ever change your ways and try to be decent.

He didn't sweat those drops of blood because of any physical suffering. It wasn't because of any fear of death, for if Jesus had been afraid to die He would have been a coward, and He wasn't a coward, although He was willing to die if God said to. I don't want to die. I want to stay here as long as I can. And so did Jesus, but He wasn't afraid to die. No. It was because of His grief for man.

A great martyr said as he stood in the midst of the flames that were devouring him: "Though you see the flesh fall from my bones I absolutely feel no pain."

If you ever had any doubt about a literal Hell, a fiery Hell, where the wicked must remain forever, it would all vanish as I see Jesus Christ in Gethsemane, agonizing because men would not accept Him and were going to Hell.

Hell must be an awful place. The fact that God went to the trouble He did to send Jesus Christ to this earth and to work out His great plan of redemption proves that it must be an awful place. I think this should give us a new vision.

Yes, it was a bitter cup for Jesus. Oh, don't be careless professors of Christianity for another minutes. Don't you start to make a cold, formal prayer when you come to address Almighty God! Don't you dare to regard this Campaign in a critical and carping way. Oh, Hell must be an awful place when Jesus was in such agony to think that men were going there. You're a big fool to go to Hell, but it will be your own fault if you do. God doesn't want you to go there, but He can't stop you. He has sacrificed His son to keep you out of Hell, and what more could He do? I am doing all I can to keep you out of Hell. I have stood here and preached to you and I've done all that I could, and if you won't be saved, all right -- go to Hell.

When Jesus was being led out to be sacrificed women followed Him and wept, and He turned to them and said: "Daughters of Jerusalem, weep not for me, but weep for yourselves and for your children." For He said, "For if they do these things in a green tree, what shall be done in the dry?" Jesus meant that they shouldn't weep for Him, but for those who were about to crucify Him; He meant that there were more reasons to weep for them than to weep for Him.

So don't weep for others' troubles; weep for your own soul. Don't worry about my vocabulary, sister; get on your knees and pray for your salvation, Don't worry about my eccentricities; you'd better look after your own faults.

We learn still another lesson - the power of prayer.

Every man and every woman that God has used to halt this sin cursed world and set it going Godward has been a Christian of prayer. Martin Luther arose from his bed and prayed at night, and when the break of day came he called his wife and said to her, "It has come." History records that on that very day King Charles granted religious toleration, a thing for which Luther had prayed.

John Knox, whom his queen feared more than any other man, was in such agony of prayer that he ran out into the street and fell on his face and cried, "Oh, God, give me Scotland or I'll die." And God gave him Scotland, and not only that, He threw England in for good measure.

When Jonathan Edwards was about to preach his greatest sermon on "Sinners in the Hands of an Angry God," he prayed for days- and when he stood before his congregation and preached it, men caught at the seat in their terror, and some fell to the floor; and the people cited out in their fear, "Mr. Edwards, tell us how we can be saved!"

I believe that if you will pray as you ought to pray, you will have more people at the altar in the next week than you have had in all the weeks that are passed. You have never had the people of this community in such a frame of mind as they are in now, and you may never have things as they now are again. Now is the time to save souls. If you can't save them now, God pity you, for you never will.

An old infidel - a blacksmith - said that he could refute any argument that a Christian could make. There was an old deacon there - he was a Baptist, and he heard of it. He told his wife and they got down on their knees and prayed until 3 o'clock in the morning. That morning the old deacon hitched up and drove over to see the man. He went into the blacksmith shop and the infidel was standing there, and the deacon stood before him. He said, "My wife and I prayed for you until 3 o'clock this morning." Then his eyes filled with tears and he sobbed and turned away. He couldn't think of one of the arguments he had prepared. He drove back home, and when he got there he said to his wife, "I've made an old fool of myself. It was all for nothing. When I saw him I just told him that we had been praying for him, then I broke down and couldn't think of another thing, and came home".

In the meantime the infidel went into his own house and he said to his wife: "I heard a new argument this morning." She said, "What was that?" "Why," he said, "the old deacon drove in to see me this morning and told me that he and his wife had prayed for me until 3 o'clock in the morning. Then he sobbed and went away." And the infidel said, "I'd like to talk to him." They drove over and he told the deacon why he had come, and it was not long before the deacon had him on his knees and he was saved.

A mother had some daughters, and they were frivolous and coquettish girls. She couldn't get them to give up their pleasures and live for God. She prayed for them, and finally one day she said to them: "I'm ashamed of you. I'm almost sorry that I bore you and held you on my knees. You care more for others than you do for your God or your mother. Others ask you to go with them, and you go. I ask you to go with me, and you won't go. I'm going into my closet and I'm going to pray for you, I don't know that I shall ever come out alive."

She went in and prayed. The hours went by and still she prayed. Finally there was a knock at the door, and one of her daughters stood there. She was weeping, and she said, "Mother, I want to be saved. I've come to pray with you." So the two of them prayed and the hours went by, and presently another daughter came and joined them there; and before night came all those girls had found Jesus.

Then, we learn a lesson of the spirit of deep concern over soul.

The spirit of concern that we find in the Bible puts to shame many who are in Omaha. Some of you have been coming to this tabernacle ever since the meetings were begun, but you have simply sat here. You haven't put forth a hand to bring anyone to Christ. If you are one of these, you are absolutely worthless so far as God is concerned. You are of no use to him and he looks on you as an unprofitable servant. How can you sit by while souls are going to Hell? What are you going to say to God about it after a while? Go and see an unsaved person die, and read the obituary not once, but twice, and realize that he died unsaved, and then see what you think of it!

Someone may say, "How do I know how God feels about it?" How do I know whether he is really concerned over sinners? I know it. It would be a sin of presumption if I did not. If God cared as little for the souls of men as some of you care, not a soul ever would have been saved - it is not possible for the human mind to have a greater conception of God than is revealed to us in Jesus Christ. For a man to say he loves God and then turn his back on Jesus Christ is an insult to the Almighty. You will find in Him just what your heart has been looking for, and you'll find it nowhere else.

I can see Jesus in the Garden looking down on Jerusalem and saying, "Oh, Jerusalem, Jerusalem, thou that killest the prophets, and stoned them which are sent unto thee; how often would I have gathered thy children together, even as a hen gathered her chickens under her wings, and ye would not." It is a matter of history that from that day Jesus turned away from the Jews. He never appealed to them again, but turned to the Gentiles - but God's got a plan for the Jews. So Jesus is God made manifest in the flesh.

Did you ever weep over the sins of the people? Did you ever weep over the evil of the multitude? If you never did then there's something wrong with your religion. If God Almighty had no more concern about the salvation of Omaha than some of you, Omaha would have been in Hell long ago. If God were no more anxious about Omaha than some of the preachers I could name, this city would have been damned long ago. I've been here long enough to see that.

Salvation all comes through Jesus. You've got to see Jesus in order to see God, and you've got to see God in order to enter Heaven. The hope of the world is in Jesus Christ. The hope of America is in Christ, not in free trade; it's not in the banking system, it's not in tariff reform, or conservation of natural resources or the ship problem or universities. We need a great tidal wave of religion.

One time I found a little boy in the street. After that boy had been restored to his mother, I found that the mother had been frantic for his return. She could not do enough to show her appreciation. It opened my eyes and I said, "God, I know how you feel about all this unsaved world, for I know how that mother felt over that little lost boy."

Another lesson we find is that much concern moves the unsaved for God.

Much concern is aroused by prayer. Doctor Chapman told me that when he was a young minister and was pastor of a little Dutch Presbyterian church in New York state, he started what he called a Revival. He told me that he had often apologized to God since then for calling it that. He would preach, and then he would say, "If anyone would like to join the Church, let them step in and meet the session." If that isn't as cold-blooded a proposition as you can find, I'll give it up. Nobody stepped in to meet the session. They didn't believe in excitement in the church. No, sir. If anybody wanted to join he could step in and meet the session.

Doctor Chapman became concerned for one young man. He felt that he ought to speak for him, but he feared that he might show more zeal than knowledge. He felt the man might be offended if he went to him in that way. He had the wrong idea. If anyone is offended because you try to do right, let them go, If anyone is offended because you ask them to he a Christian, let them go to Hell. You've done your duty. He thought it over and made up his mind to speak that very night. The young man did not come that night, so on the next day Doctor Chapman drove out in a cutter to see him. He met the man and said, "I want you to be a Christian."

The man was angry. He said, "You blankety-blank little preacher, I don't want you to come to me about that." Doctor Chapman turned and left him and drove away. He caught cold while driving out there and it stayed with him that winter, and soon after he left the place and took up Evangelistic work.

One night ten years after, he was holding a meeting at Saratoga, when he saw a man coming down the aisle.

"Don't you know me?" the man asked. Doctor Chapman didn't know him.

"Why," the man said, "I'm Benedict from Schuylerville. I'm the man who cursed you when you drove out to my home and asked me to be a Christian. I want to be a Christian now."

"What has changed you?" Doctor Chapman asked.

"I'll tell you," said the man. "I never heard a sermon that touched me, nor a song. It was your tears, the tears that were in your eyes as I cursed you and you turned away. I've never been able to forget them. I've never had a day's peace since that moment."

Oh, if you knew the power of tears for the sinner. If you only felt enough concern to weep over those who are in danger of being lost. The sight of such tears would win many souls for Christ.

One morning when I was over in Iowa a young woman came to my door and knocked and said that a man wanted to see me. I found that he was a Church member - a ruling elder. He told me that he had not been living right. "How can I get right?" he asked.

I told him that his confession must be as public as his sin had been great. I told him that he would have to stand up and tell the people that he hadn't been living right and promise that with God's help he would do better. He said, "Oh, I can't do that."

"All right," I said, "but if you aren't willing to do what you must do to get right, what did you come to me for?"

He finally said he would do it, and he did. Then he asked me to pray for him and I did. Then he asked me to pray for his son Ernest, and I prayed for him at intervals that day. The boy was at Shenandoah, that was in western Iowa - going to school. He didn't go with his class that day. Late that night there was a knock at the door and when they opened it, Ernest was there. He had walked sixteen or seventeen miles to get home and he was almost frozen.

"What's wrong?" the father asked.

"Oh, father, I'm an awful sinner," said the boy.

They called his mother and they got him warm. Today he is preaching the gospel to the heathen. God shot the arrow of conviction over fifteen miles that day in answer to our prayers.

If the Church people get right, the whole world will get right. The world is challenging the Church instead of the Church challenging the world. If it was as easy to get the Church on its knees as it is to get the unsaved world into the kingdom, we wouldn't have any more trouble about religion. And God can't save you unless you're willing. He won't coerce you to it.

I often think of what Bob Ingersoll might have been if he had only been turned into Christianity. What a power for God that man could have been!

I often think of what a power Voltaire could have been for God - that brilliant man over whose writings many have stumbled to Hell.

Carey translated the Bible into twenty-four languages and dialects.

Finney brought over 1,000,000 into the Kingdom of God.

Moody brought hundreds of thousands to Christ.

I have never seen a minister who preached doctrines and creeds and evolution and all such things who had any real concern for the souls of his people. Jesus Christ is in a hurry to save this world and there never was an age when people were so hungry for the truth as they are today.

The angels don't care anything about a railroad in Alaska. What do the angels care about political principles? What do they care about a forty story skyscraper or reclaiming the deserts of the west? What do they care about pictures, art or science? The only thing they're interested in is the salvation of man. If you want to make the bells of Heaven ring, get down on your knees. Tell a sinner about Jesus Christ if you want to hear the Heavenly bells. Nothing will swing open the prison doors and bring men out of sin like prayer.

I never see a man or a woman or boy or girl but I do not think that God has a plan for them, and wonder what it is. He has a plan for each of us. He will use each of us to His glory if we will only let Him. We can defeat His plan if we want to.

Finally, we find that God honors this spirit in deep concern for the unsaved. This concern comes from a clear realization of man's relation. I never knew a higher critical preacher to save them from Hell. Such preaching is not of God and He will not bless it. It is of the devil. If you haven't got in your heart an agonized concern for the unsaved go right down there in front and fall in the sawdust and ask God to forgive you.

Nothing makes such joy in Heaven as the salvation of a soul. The angels don't care a rap about your wealth; they don't care about your social position, they don't care about your culture. It's the salvation of sinners the angels care about.

He That Winneth Souls is Wise

"He that winneth souls is wise."

Proverbs 11:30

• • •

There are vast multitudes in this enlightened land of ours who are in open rebellion against God. "We will not have this man, Jesus Christ, to reign over us," is the heartless cry that winds its flight from office, shop, store, factory, home, college, and the busy mart of trade. Lots of people are willing, my friends, to accept whatever they want from the Bible. They would like to codify it; they would like to sit down and eliminate that which isn't pleasant to them to receive and which they don't like to adjust their lives to, and insert something they would like. You take it as it is given, and if you don't, you will go to Hell. God almighty won't adjust His principles to suit the opinions of anybody. The Lord has made His revelation known to the world, and it is up to you and not to the Lord. He has done all He ever will or can do to save this world. He has given sunshine and rain and ground; it is up to you to plant the seed, to plow it or starve to death. God has done His part; He will do no more.

Church and Business Fail Because They Have No Definite Aim

They say they will give us the Sermon on the Mount, or the Decalogue, minus the things that they don't like. They say, "We have no king but self"; and the only law that multitudes of people recognize is the law of their own desires and ambitions. They do the thing because they personally want to do it, and they do not give a rap what influence it has upon their character of what influence their conduct has upon others who are looking to them for an example. All the law they know is the law of their own desire. That's all!

"And so our Lord is now rejected; And by the world disowned. By the many still neglected, But by the few enthroned."

That is true of the denominations that are represented in these meetings, too. Out in a western state four years ago a report was made that during that year (there were 300 churches of that denomination in that state and they spent $300,000 for current expenses) they held 46,000 meetings and during the year there were just 87 men and women converted and joined those churches on confession of faith. I suppose that is this safe and sane evangelism that I hear so much about. It wouldn't take the world long to get into Hell if that is all there is to it! In Chicago just a few years ago the church made a report. There was an average of five who joined each church on confession of faith -- some more, some less -- but it averaged five for a year. And the last year 7,5000 churches of all denominations made reports and not one accession that year on confession of faith. All right, look at it! Just face the conditions and you will see why probably I talk in a way that grates on your nerves, but you will realize that I am only telling you the truth.

Now, what is lacking? Why these meager results? Why the expenditure of so much energy and time and money? It is because there is not a definite effort put forth to persuade a definite person to accept a definite Saviour at a definite time -- and that time is NOW. That is the whole thing in a nutshell, boiled down to one sentence. That is why we are not making headway.

But wait! This element of failure is not simply confined to the church. Ninety-nine per cent of the businessmen fail. A banker told me in Chicago that forty years ago there were one hundred business houses, any one of whose paper would have passed without protest, and today only four of those houses were named. The rest of them have been ruined, gone into bankruptcy, gone out of business. There were four of them after forty years and they all passed without protest at any bank.

Only about three men out of a thousand succeed. Seventy five percent of the lawyers who graduate from law school fail to make good. Sixty five percent of the physicians fail to make good. The failure of these three classes is due largely to the lack of definite, systematic work. No political battle is won on the stump. It is not the spellbinders from the rear end of a special train who turn the vote. Sometimes a bleary-eyed, bloated-faced, bull-necked, whiskey-soaked, tinhorn politician will win more votes than the most silver-tongued spellbinder who ever spouted the principles from the rear end of a special train.

Now to give you an illustration. New York State used to be the pivot state in the presidential election. It isn't anymore. They don't care how New York goes anymore. But it used to be "As goes New York." Everybody knows that the State of New York is Republican. Everybody knows that the city of New York is Democratic. In the State the Republican party figures that it must have about 125,000 or 150,000 majority to overcome the Democratic majority in New York. So when Ben Harrison and Grover Cleveland ran for President in 1888, they went to work. They took the city, divided it, and subdivided it until they got it down into blocks. They had a man over every section and every subdivision, and they had the leading businessmen of the city in those places.

Those men used to meet every day. They used to pound this into them: "You are not responsible for who is elected; you are not responsible for who goes to Washington, Harrison or Cleveland. You are not responsible who carries this state, this city; but you are responsible to know every man in your block and to know how he votes, and if he votes." They kept pounding that one thing into the men -- "Know the block! Know the block!"

They watched the town, and when the votes were counted, Ben Harrison went to Washington instead of Grover Cleveland. That was the way they put it over.

Now that is what Jesus Christ said. In other words, men will work harder to win in business and politics than the church will in religion. I am disgusted with them all! You think you can just open your church door and ring a church bell and people will come. That has been going on long enough. The church has got to wake up and do something.

You simply think that because the calendar announces that it is the Lord's day that that is all you have to do, and that if you put on a little better dress and look a little more pious that that is serving the Lord, and you go to the Devil six days in the week.

I know of a varnish company in this country that pays a man ten thousand dollars a year to look nice. He is a good dresser; he is a good mixer. He has a smile that doesn't come off. He never tries to sell varnish, but he paves the way for the fellow who comes from the firm to sell the varnish to the big railroads and the big institutions that buy it. All he does is just sort of win their friendship and make it easy for the guy who does sell the varnish. They pay him ten thousand a year just for that.

That is the way people do in order to succeed in business. What is the church doing to win people for Christ? I bet alot of you don't know whether or not people right around in your neighborhood are Christians. We never do anything; no wonder the world is going to the Devil.

Soul Winning, the Most Effective Work in the World

Another thing; it is the simplest and most effective work in the world. Andrew wins Peter; Peter turns around and wins three thousand at Pentecost.

Years ago a man went into a shoe store in Boston and found a young fellow selling shoes and boots. He talked to him about Jesus Christ and won him for Christ. The name of that little boy was Dwight L. Moody. Do you know the name of the man who won Moody for Christ? I don't suppose there are five people in this audience who do. His name was Kimball. God used Kimball to win Moody, but He used Moody to win the multitude.

Andrew didn't have sense enough to win the multitude, but Peter did. That is the way God works! Oh, I get so sick of people being dead! You have sat around so long you have mildewed.

The Earl of Shaftsbury, who gave sixty-five years of his life working among the costermongers, the fallen, the submerged and mudsills of London, was won to Jesus Christ by a servant girl in his home. He was wavering, going down the line with the gang of young bloods when his father died. This servant girl, a godly girl, said "You inherit all the honor and all the wealth that goes along with the name of Shaftsbury, but are you going to a premature grave because of the way you are going, the life you are living, and bring disgrace upon your father's memory and your mother's?" The Earl of Shaftsbury, when he was eighteen years old, fell on his knees and gave his heart to Jesus Christ. When he died, his funeral was the greatest ever held in England except when a king or queen had died.

See what she did? She won him to the Lord and then the Lord took him and used him to win the multitudes. Charles G. Finney, after learning the name of a man or a woman, invariably asked, "Are you a Christian?"

The Soul-Winning Work of John Vassar

John Vassar was one of the greatest personal workers of the nineteenth century. He never preached a sermon but that he did personal work. He was a wonder. One time he was going to help a preacher in a town. This preacher met Vassar at the Depot. Walking down to the hotel they went past a blacksmith shop. He said to Vassar, "There's a blacksmith in there. He's got a great drag with his crowd but he never comes to church. If we could only win him, then he would win scores in his class." Vassar asked, "Have you talked to him?" "Oh, we are afraid. He will cuss any preacher who comes near him." He said, "Wait a minute until I take my turn." Vassar went in. The man was shoeing a mule -- that isn't a good time to talk religion to a man, take it from me! But Vassar had good sense and waited until the fellow was through and had disarmed his prejudice. In fifteen minutes he had him on his knees weeping like a child. He went up to the hotel where he was to be entertained . He registered, then strolled around, looking for somebody to speak to. He went into a little reception room and there sat a finely dressed lady. He walked up to her and said, "Lady, are you a Christian?" She said, "Yes, I am." "I beg your pardon," he said, "I didn't mean that kind. I mean, have you been born again?"

"Oh," she said, "we've gotten over that here in Boston." "Well," he said, "lady, you've gotten over Jesus Christ in Boston, too. You've gotten over God." He talked with her until her prejudice was disarmed and tears trickled down her cheeks; then he said, "May I pray for you?" She said, "I wish you would. God knows I need it, although I'm a member of the church."

He prayed. She wept and he slipped out. Her husband came in and noticed that her eyes were red. He said, "Has anybody insulted you?" She said, "The queerest little man was here a little while ago and he talked so nice to me about Jesus." He said, "If I had been here I would have told him to go along and mind his business." She said, "I wish you had been here. You would have thought he was minding his business. His business was a mission for his King, to bring people to Jesus Christ."

Vassar distributed tracts in the army. He worked with the American Bible Society. When the chaplain died, they wanted Vassar to take the place of the chaplain. He wasn't ordained and the government law does not allow anybody to be a chaplain who hasn't been ordained. He came up to Poughkeepsie and they were examining him. One fellow with cinders all over his back, said, "Mr. Vassar, your duty now is to distribute tracts. Your salary is three hundred dollars a year, and you wish to be ordained?"

"Yes, sir."

"Does that mean an increase of salary?"

"Yes, sir, fifteen hundred dollars a year."

Then he said, "The increase of salary has allured you and brought you here for us to ordain."

Vassar said, "Stop where you are! I don't want it; I won't take it if you give it to me", and he wouldn't. He went back to distributing tracts for three hundred dollars a year, to do something for Jesus Christ. He was a wonder. God did marvelous things through him.

"Are you lonesome?" a man asked a lighthouse keeper. "Are you lonesome out on this lonesome spot?" He said, "I was before I saved four men from drowning...Is that a boat out there?" He was always on the lookout for other boats that he might save men from a watery grave.

Get somebody else for Jesus Christ and you will get a new vision of life, a new vision of what it means. It is something besides going to church and keeping warm a little spot seventeen inches square for a half hour and listening to a sermonette. You had better squirm around in your seat and stoop down! You had better duck!

"He that winneth souls is wise." Some people think it is beneath their dignity. Then you live on a higher plane than your Master, for He went about doing good wherever he was in the world.

A lady said to a friend of mine, "Do you think that my blindness will hinder me?" My friend answered, "It is a misfortune, but I don't know. I have the opinion it will be a help to you, because people will come up to you to express their sympathy for your lack of sight and that will give you the opportunity to speak of Jesus."

"Oh," she said, "I don't mean in an effort like that, but to stand on the platform." She thought the only way to serve God was to get in the spotlight, not to be doing something with the people whom she might shake hands with day by day in her home.

A man was thinking of entering evangelistic work. He came to my friend, Dr. Chapman, and said, "I am thinking of entering evangelistic work."

"That's good." Dr. Chapman said.

"I think I will begin out in Colorado -- Denver and Colorado Springs, and out in Pasadena, California. My relatives are there."

My friend said, "Have you any brothers or sisters?"

"Yes, I have."

"Are they Christians?"

"Well," he said, "I don't know. When we set up the estate four years ago my brother and I had a quarrel over it and we haven't spoken since."

"And your sister?"

"My sister took my brother's views of the proposition and she hasn't spoken to me since. I haven't been in her home."

Dr. Chapman said, "What do you intend to do?"

He said, "Evangelistic work."

Dr. Chapman said, "The Bible says, 'First be reconciled to thy brother.' If you start out the way you are, failure is written all over you. 'If I regard iniquity in my heart, the Lord will not hear me,' the Bible tells me, so there is no use trying to bother your head about God for He won't listen to you. That's as sure as you live."

Soul Winning is Difficult Work

Now, it is a difficult form of work. It is more difficult than preaching; it is more difficult than attending conventions; more difficult than giving goods to the poor. (When you do give goods to the poor, don't wait until the moths have eaten holes in them. And when you give them away, don't cut off all the buttons and braid. Poor folks like them as well as you do. It is no act of charity when you have taken off all you want, then turned the rest over to somebody else. No, no! Then angles never record an act like that.) You will never see it when you get to Heaven if you have an easy time. Oh, you can pin on a badge, usher people to their seats, pass the collection plate, be an elder or a deacon or a steward; you can go to church, sing in the choir, be a member of a Home or Foreign Missionary Society -- the Devil will even let you attend Bible conferences -- but the minute you begin to do personal work, to try to get somebody to take a stand for Christ, all the devils in Hell will be on your back, for they know that is a challenge to the Devil and to his forces. And I hope that the work of leading people to Christ by personal effort will always be hard. I have no sympathy for folks who are looking for something easy!

I preached out in Salida, Colorado, a few years ago. The city lies 8,5000 feet on one of the spurs of the Rocky Mountains. There was a woman there who sang in the choir. I used to drive them out when they went to speak to somebody about Jesus Christ. One day she came to me and said, "Mr. Sunday, will you speak to my husband about being a Christian?"

I said, "Have you spoken to him?"

She said, "No."

I said, "No madam, I will not."

She said, "Why?"

I said, "God wants you to go and you are trying to sidestep and get me to do it."

I said, "You go speak to him and if you can't win him for Christ, come and tell me, then I will go."

"Well," she said, "you would have a greater influence with him than I have."

"How long have you been married?" I asked." Five years." I said, "I have been in this town three weeks and it is a compliment for you to say that to me. You have cooked for him and sewed on buttons for him for five years."

Finally one night, she said, "Isn't it hot?" I said to her, "You like to sing in the choir, don't you?" She said, "I love to do that." "You don't like to do personal work?" I asked. "Then your idea of serving God is to pick out the things you would like to do, and the things that you don't like to do you let somebody else do; then you let it go at that." I said, "Then you will forget every blessing that ever came to you."

One night I drove her off the platform; later I saw her coming down the aisle. Her husband sat on the front seat. She slipped her arm around his neck and whispered something in his ear. He nodded his head and down the aisle he came. He turned to her and said, "Bess, I've been waiting for weeks for you to ask me that."

I was out in Colorado Springs not very long ago and she came up to Denver. I said, "How do you do, Mrs. C." "How do you do?" I said, "Where's Charlie?" "He went to heaven two years ago, but he prayed and lived consistently until the hour that God called him."

Get out and do something! "He isn't my boy." That same spirit of letting people go to the Devil because they don't eat at your table and because you are not married to them -- there is too much of that today in the world." He that winneth souls is wise."

God Blesses Personal Effort

A mother in a home had a magnificent character. To my knowledge there had never been a stranger enter that home for years that she hadn't talked to him about Jesus Christ. She was bemoaning the fact that she couldn't do anything or wasn't doing anything for the Lord, yet she was doing more practical Christian work, consistently every day, than the entire membership of that church of five hundred people. She was doing more!

So it the personal effort that God will honor and that God will bless. And listen! There are fifteen million young men in this country between the ages of sixteen and thirty five. Fourteen million of them are not members of any church, Catholic or Protestant. Seven million of them attend church regularly. Nine million of them never darken a church door from one year's end to another.

After the Iroquois Theater fire in Chicago where six hundred people burned to death, a girl about seventeen years of age fought her way through the great torrents of blood and crushed and charred and baked flesh. Her hair was singed, her eyebrows were burned off, her face and hands were blistered, her clothing was hanging in charred rags. As she got on the street car to go home she was moaning and sighing. She would wring her hands and say "O, God! O, God!" A lady next to her said, "Well, you ought to be thankful that you got out alive." She said, "I am, but I didn't help anybody else out! It was all I could do to get out." What she was moaning about was the fact that others had to die because she didn't help them. Yet she was sitting by people who had not thought of others -- letting them go to Hell.

Oh, he that winneth souls is wise! Is wise! You would feel different, perhaps, if it were some of your own, but remember, if it is not your flesh and blood it is somebody else's.

Out in Pennsylvania they had a mine cave-in. The alarm was sounded and men came and volunteered. With pick and shovel they worked, trying to dig quickly to the men lest they die. Up tottered an old man seventy-five years old. He threw off his cap, coat and vest, spit on his hands, and picking up the pick, he picked and picked. Then he got the shovel and he shoveled until the sweat rolled down his cheeks. He stood tottering, about ready to fall. Some of the younger men said to him, "Grandpa, get away and let us young fellows do this."

He said, "Great God, boys! I've got three sons down in there! I must do something!" And if it isn't your boy, it is somebody else's. If it isn't your girl, it is somebody else's.

That is the trouble with the world today. We don't care a rap what becomes of others so long as we go through the world. Now you may soon go; you may die and they may die; and you may live and they may die, but no matter whether you go first or last, you have to meet at the judgment. That is settled! You have to do that.

A casket containing the body of a beautiful seventeen year old girl with the dew of youth on her brow, was being borne from the church to the graveyard. The girl's friends stood around the grave. As they lowered the coffin, a Sunday school teacher who stood there shrieked and screamed and wrung her hands in grief. After the carriage was driven away and after things had been cleared up, the minister went to see this girl. He said, "I noticed your hysteric grief at the grave. Was she a Christian?" The Sunday school teacher said, "I noticed her growing careless with her companions and going into questionable places." Then the girl said to the minister, "I was sure you'd speak to her, for you know more about those things." He said, "No, I didn't speak to her. I intended to but," he said, "I didn't. I was sure you would. She was a girl and you were a girl and you better understood one another. Let's go and see her mother."

The minister and the Sunday school teacher went and talked with the girl's mother. She said, "Yes, I noticed it. I used to plead with her, but she would get mad at me, thinking I was interfering with her company. I hope you spoke to her."

Neither of them had, and she had gone to wait at the judgment bar, to witness against the three -- her mother, the preacher, and the Sunday school teacher, for they said nothing. "He that winneth souls is wise!" He is wise!

So there must be a confession of sin. The sin of neglect -- confess that; and the sin of unforgiveness, the sin of indifference. David said, "If I regard iniquity in my heart, the Lord will not hear me." Oh, you get the light of Jesus in your heart! Jesus Christ is able, my friend, to reveal Himself to the agnostic, materialist, like He did to Balaam until he knew Jesus Christ. Oh, He can flash the deity of Jesus Christ into the brain of the son of an orthodox Unitarian of New England, as He did the son of Edward Everett Hale. He is able to knock the scales from the credulous worshipers of Mary Baker Glover Eddy until you will find that matter is existent and not an illusion of the mortal mind.

What God Did Through the Testimony of an Fourteen Year Old Boy

He that winneth souls is wise! My friend, Dr. Broughton, used to be pastor of a big Baptist church in Atlanta, Georgia. When he was a young minister he went out to help a pastor in revival meetings. He said he would ask God to forgive him a good many times. He said he went and preached and he never in all his days saw such a dead, lifeless, indifferent, apathetic crowd. He didn't believe there was such a crowd this side of the cemetery. He said he preached. Nobody smiled. They all looked like epitaphs on a tombstone. He said he asked for a show of hands; nobody would lift them. He would ask for a request for prayer; nobody would appeal. To every appeal they were as deaf as Hades. He was discouraged about it. One time he made an appeal and said, "If there is a man here who wants us to pray, a father who wants us to pray for his children, lift your hand."

A boy, fourteen years of age, who sat on the end of the seat, raised his hand. He said, "If there is a mother here who wants us to pray for her child, or children, lift your hand." The boy lifted his hand. He said, "If there is a businessman here who has interests that concern his partner, lift your hand." Up went the boy's hand. He made the appeal governing both sexes. He said to himself, "This child's a monstrosity." He said, "I have made an appeal covering both sexes and all ages. To every appeal he has lifted his hand." He went back to the hotel. Sitting in his chair he heard a rap at the door. "Come in!" In walked one of the deacons, stroking his long bird-tail whiskers.

"How do you do, Deacon?"

He said, "We ain't having much of a meeting."

"Never saw anything worse."

"I thought I'd come up and tell you about that little boy who's down to the church," the deacon said. "What do you mean?" Dr. Broughton asked. "Well, every time you make an appeal, he lifts his hand. He's just making a fool of you."

"Forget it. He's making a fool of you and all the rest of the fools who profess to be Christians." The deacon said, "Well, I thought I'd come and tell you so you could tell him to stay away." Dr. Broughton said, "I'll give that boy ten dollars a day to come. He's the only evidence of life I've seen in the city. If you think I'm going to turn the hose on him, you've got another guess coming."

"Well," the deacon said, "I thought I'd tell you." Stroking his whiskers, he went out. Dr. Broughton went on to preach and make similar appeals. The only one who would respond was that boy. Up would go his hand. Another day he heard a knock. "Come in!" In came this old deacon. He said, "Do you know that boy?"

"Certainly I know him; he's the only one I do know." He said, "You ain't having much of a revival." He said, "No, you need an undertaker in this town instead of an evangelist. You are the deadest crowd that I have ever seen. And if God or anybody else had told me that there was such a dead, indifferent membership on earth, I wouldn't have believed it."

"Well," the deacon said, "do you know that boy ain't overly bright?" "He's got you backed off the boards. He's got sense enough to make a response," replied Dr. Broughton. "Well," he said, "I thought I'd tell you." The preacher said, "You don't need to tell me." The pastor came to Dr. Broughton and said, "Doctor, before I was sure that you were coming to preach on Sunday morning for a brother minister in another city who is away and I'd like to have you preach for me on Sunday morning." He said, "Very well." On Saturday night he heard a rap at the door. "Come in!" In came this old deacon, stroking his whiskers. "Howdy, Doc." "How do you do, Deacon?" He said, "The domine asked (they always call the preacher the domine) -- the domine asked you to preach on Sunday morning, didn't he?" "Yes." He said, "Now, don't you ask for converts because there ain't any."

"Deacon, look me in the face, if you can, and answer me this: You knew that if I did, there would be one or some and you don't want that one, or some, to join the church." He squirmed uncomfortably. "Well", he said, "you can do as you please." He said, "I'd do that without your consent. I'll preach if I feel God and the Spirit; if I don't, I won't. I won't do it because you told me to do it, or not to do it. Neither would I do it if you asked me to or if you asked me not to." Sunday morning he walked out and preached. When he got through he said, "If there is anybody here who wants to be a Christian, wants to join the church, come down and take me by the hand." Pretty soon there was a shuffling and down the aisle came that boy. Dr. Broughton took him by the hand and said, "Sit down, sonny." He asked the usual questions. The child gave answers and Dr. Broughton repeated the answers. He said to the audience, "You have all heard the questions I have asked and the answers given, for I have repeated both. All who are in favor of giving this boy the right hand of fellowship and receiving him in full membership, say 'aye'". Two farmers voted aye and the rest of them kept quiet. Dr. Broughton said, "The ayes have it." He got the kid up on the platform and baptized him.

The boy went bounding home. He lived with his grandfather since his mother was dead. His grandfather was an invalid, and the richest man in that section of Georgia. For nearly sixty years he had never been known to darken a church door. He was a leader of the infidels; he denounced religion because of unbelief, and blatantly spewed out the theories and doctrines of infidelity. The boy bounded in, put his arms around the old man's neck and said, "Grandpa, they took me into the church, and Dr. Broughton baptized me, and if you will come up there, they will take you in, too." He said, "Go away, son, don't bother me. Grandpa don't care about it." He pushed the boy off, but back in again he came. He kept begging his grandpa to go, but he said, "Don't bother your grandpa; go on away." He said, "Grandpa, I'll tell you what they will ask you, and I'll tell you what to say. Come on and go." My friend preached to men only on Sunday afternoon. They saw this boy come into the church leading his old grandfather, who was hobbling on the crutches of decrepitude as he came down the aisle. He sat down and listened.

When my friend got through the grandfather arose and said, "Dr. Broughton, may I speak a few words?" He stood trembling on his cane. "I have cussed and damned God all my life. This is the first time I have crossed a church threshold for over sixty years. My little grandson -- and you know he ain't overly bright; his ma's gone and he lives with me and his grandma -- he came home and said you took him into the church and told me if I'd come you'd take me in. Dr. Broughton, if you think God will reach down and take an old reprobate like me, who has cussed Him all my days, and I've never, never prayed -- if you think the Lord will take me in the sunset of life and kiss away the stains of guilt, I'd like to come."

Dr. Broughton said, "Him that cometh to me I will in no wise cast out."

The old man came hobbling down and said, "I have wandered far away from God, but now I'm coming home."

He was baptized and received into the church. Listen! They went home. The next day, the little boy went bounding downtown into a saloon kept by his father. He said, "O papa, grandpa and me have joined the church and if you'll come up, they will take you in. I will tell you what they will ask you and I'll tell you what to say." He said, "Go out of here, my son; this is no place for you." Say, if a dirty, stinking saloon is no place for my boy, it's no place for me. If it's good for me, it's good for him, and if it's bad for him, it's bad for me. To Hell with the saloon!

He said to him, "Go on out of here, son. Go on out of here. This is no place for a boy." "Pa, come on. They will take you in."

Listen! The next Sunday that man walked down the aisle, told the story of what his little boy had done, and he said "If you think that God can save a saloon-keeper, I'd like to be a Christian."

He joined the church, then he said, "Come down tomorrow morning and we will break the bottles of whiskey and champagne and beer." They brought them into the street and they did. They turned it into the sewer as the people stood singing. He said, "I feel that my mission is to the saloon-keepers of that part of the country."

He started out and by personal effort, with drunkards and saloon-keepers, started a tidal wave of religion. And the first county that went dry in Georgia was that county. The state was put dry by the legislative enactment, and they never had a saloon in that county from that day till this. It all started with that little boy.

You've got as much sense as the boy, haven't you? Go do likewise; that is my message.

Motherhood

"Take this child away, and nurse it for me, and I will give thee thy wages."

Exodus 2:9

• • •

THE STORY OF MOSES is one of the most beautiful and fascinating in all the world. It takes a hold on us and never for an instant does it lose its interest, for it is so graphically told that once heard it is never forgotten.

I have often imagined the anxiety with which that child was born, for he came into the world with the sentence of death lagging over him, for Pharaoh had decreed that the male children should die, and the mother defied even the command of the king, and determined that the child should live, and right from the beginning the battle of right against might was fought at the cradle.

Moses' mother was a slave. She had to work in the brick yards or labor in the field, but God was on her side and she won, as the mother always wins with God on her side. Before going to work she had to choose some hiding place for her child, and she put his little sister, Miriam, on guard while she kept herself from being seen by the soldiers of Pharaoh, who were seeking everywhere to murder the Jewish male children.

For three months she kept him hidden, possibly finding a new hiding place every few days. It is hard to imagine anything more difficult than to hide a healthy, growing baby, and he was hidden for three months.

Now he was grown larger and more full of life and a more secure hiding place had to be found, and I can imagine this mother giving up her rest and sleep to prepare an ark for the saving of her child.

I believe the plan must have been formulated in Heaven. I have often thought God must have been as much interested in that work as was the mother of Moses, for you can't make me believe that an event so important as that and so far-reaching in its results ever happened by luck or by chance.

Possibly God whispered the plan to the mother when she went to Him in prayer and in her grief because she was afraid the sword of Pharaoh would murder her child. And how carefully the material out of which the ark was made had to be selected!

I think every twig was carefully scrutinized in order that nothing poor might get into its composition, and in the weaving of that ark, the mother's heart, her soul, her prayers, her tears, were interwoven. Oh, if you mothers would exercise as much care over the company your children keep, over the books they read and the places they go, there would not be so many girls feeding the red light district, nor so many boys growing up to bad, criminal lives.

And with what thanksgiving she must have poured out her heart when at last the work was done and the ark was ready to carry its precious cargo, more precious than if it was to hold the crown jewels of Egypt. And I can imagine the last night that baby was in the home.

Probably some of you can remember when the last night came when baby was alive; you can remember the last night the coffin stayed, and the next day the pallbearers and the hearse came. The others may have slept soundly, but there was no sleep for you, and I can imagine there was no sleep for Moses' mother.

There are whips and tops and pieces of string
And shoes that no little feet ever wear -
There are bits of ribbon and broken wings
And tresses of golden hair,

There are dainty jackets that never are worn,
There are toys and models of ships;
There are books and pictures all faded and torn,
And marked by finger tips
Of dimpled hands that have fallen to dust -
Yet we strive to think that the Lord is just.

Yet a feeling of bitterness fills our souls;
Sometimes we try to pray,
That the reaper has spared so many flowers
And taken ours away.
And we sometimes doubt if the Lord can know
How our riven hearts did love them so.

But we think of our dear ones dead,
Our children who never grow old,
And how they are waiting and watching for us
In the city with streets of gold.
And how they are safe through all the years
From sickness and want and war.
We thank the great God, with falling tears,
For the things in the cabinet drawer.

Others in the house might have slept, but not a moment could she spare of the precious time allotted her with her little one, and all through the night she must have prayed that God would shield and protect her baby and bless the work she had done and the step she was about to take.

Some people often say to me: "I wonder what the angels do: how they employ their time?". I think I know what some of them did that night. You bet they were not out to some bridge whist party. They guarded that house so carefully that not a soldier of old Pharaoh ever crossed the threshold. They saw to it that not one of them harmed that baby.

At dawn the mother must have kissed him goodbye, placed him in the ark and hid him among the reeds and rushes, and with an itching heart and tear dimmed eyes she turned back again to the field and back to the brick yards to labor, and wait to see what God will do.

She had done her prayerful best, and when you have done that you can bank on it that God will not fail you. How easy it is for God to give the needed help, no matter how hopeless it might seem, if we only believe that with God all things are possible, no matter how improbable.

What unexpected answers the Lord would give to our prayers! She knew God would help her some way, but I don't think she ever dreamed that God would help her by sending Pharaoh's daughter to care for the child; but it was no harder for God to send the princess than it was to get the mother to prepare the ark. What was impossible from her standpoint was easy for God. Pharaoh's daughter came down to the water to bathe, and the ark was discovered, just as God wanted it to be, and one of her maids was sent to fetch it. You often wonder what the angels are doing. I think some of the angels herded the crocodiles on the other side of the Nile to keep them from finding Moses and eating him up.

You can bank on it all Heaven was interested to see that not one hair of that baby's head was injured. There weren't devils enough in Hell to pull one hair out of its head. You may he sure the angels were not out to some bridge whist party then. God had something for them to do.

The ark was brought, and with feminine curiosity the daughter of Pharaoh had to look into it to see what was there, and when they removed the cover there was lying a strong, healthy baby boy, kicking up its heels and sucking its thumbs, as probably most of us did when we were boys, and probably as you did when you were a girl.

The baby looks up and weeps, and those tears blotted out all that was against it and gave it a chance for its life. I don't know, but I think an angel stood there and pinched it to make it cry, for it cried at the right time. Just as God plans, God always does things at the right time. Give God a chance - I he may be a little slow at times, but He will always get around in time.

The tears of that baby were the jewels with which Israel was ransomed from Egyptian bondage. The princess had a woman's heart, and when a woman's heart and a baby's tears meet, something happens that gives the devil cold feet. Perhaps the princess had a baby that had died, and the sight of Moses may have torn the wound open and made it bleed afresh. But she had a woman's heart, and that made her forget she was the daughter of Pharaoh and she was determined to give protection to that baby.

Faithful Miriam (the Lord be praised for Miriam) saw the heart of the princess reflected in her face. Miriam had studied faces so much that she could read the princess' heart as plainly as if written in an open book, and she said to her: "Shall I go and get one of the Hebrew women to nurse the child for you?" and the princess said, "Go."

I see her little feet and legs fly as she runs down the hot, dusty road, and her mother must have seen her coming a mile away, and she ran to meet her own baby put back into her arms and she was being paid Egyptian gold to take care of her own baby.

See how the Lord does things. "Now, you take this child and nurse it for me and I will pay you your wages." It was a joke on Pharaoh's daughter, paying Moses' mother for doing what she wanted to do more than anything else - nurse her own baby.

How quickly the mother was paid for these long hours of anxiety and alarm and grief, and if the angels know what is going on what a hilarious time there must have been in Heaven when they saw Moses and Miriam back at home under the protection of the daughter of Pharaoh. I imagine she dropped on her knees and poured out her heart to God, who had helped her so gloriously. She must have said: "Well, Lord, I knew you would help me. I knew you would take care of my baby when I made the ark and put him in it and put it in the water, but I never dreamed that You would put him back into my arms to take care of, so I would not have to work and slave in the field and make back and be tortured almost to death by fear that the soldiers of Pharaoh would find my baby and kill him.

"I never thought you would soften the stony heart of Pharaoh and make him pay me for what I would rather do than anything else in this world." I expect to meet Moses' mother in Heaven, and I am going to ask her how much old Pharaoh had to pay her for the job. I think that's one of the best jokes, that old sinner having to pay the mother to take care of her own baby. But, I tell you, if you give God a chance, He will fill your heart to overflowing. Just give him a chance.

This mother had remarkable pluck. Everything was against her, but she would not give up. Her heart never failed. She made as brave a fight as any man ever made at the sound of cannon or the roar of musketry. Mothers are always brave when the safety of their children is concerned.

This incident happened out west last summer. A mother was working in a garden and the little one was playing. The mother heard the child   sitting under a tree in the yard scream; she ran, and a huge snake was wrapping its coils about the baby, and as its head swung around, she leaped and grabbed it by the neck and tore it from her baby and hurled it against a tree. She is always brave when the safety of her children is concerned.

Fathers often give up. The old man often goes to boozing, becomes dissipated, takes a dose of poison and commits suicide; but the mother will stand by the home and keep the little band together if she has to manicure her fingernails over a washboard to do it.

If men had half as much grit as the women there would be different stories written about a good many homes. Look at her work! It is the greatest in the world; in its far reaching importance it is transcendently above everything in the universe - her task in molding hearts and lives and shaping character. If you want to find greatness, don't go toward the throne; go to the cradle, and the nearer you get to the cradle, the nearer to greatness.

Now, when Jesus wanted to give His disciples an impressive object lesson, He called in a college professor, did he? Not much. He brought in a little child and said: "Except ye become as one of these, ye shall in no wise enter the kingdom of God."

The work is so important that God will not trust anybody with it but a mother. The launching of a boy or girl to live for Christ is greater work than to launch a battleship.

Moses was a chosen vessel of the Lord and God wanted him to get the right kind of a start, so He gave him a good mother. There wasn't a college professor in all Egypt that God would trust with that baby, so He put the child back in its mother's arms. He knew the best one on earth to trust with that baby was its own mother.

When God sends us great men He wants to have them get the right kind of a start. So He sees to it that they have a good mother. Most any old stick will do for a daddy. God is particular about the mothers.

And so the great need of this country or any other country is good mothers, and I believe we have more good mothers in America than any other nation on earth. If Washington's mother had been like Happy Hooligan's mother, Washington would have been a Happy Hooligan.

Somebody has said, "God could not be everywhere, so He gave us mothers." Now there may be no poetry in it, but it's true that "the hand that rocks the cradle rules the world," and if every cradle was rocked by a good mother, the world would be full of good men as sure as you breathe. If every boy and every girl today had a good mother, the saloons and disreputable houses would go out of business tomorrow.

A young man one time joined a church and the preacher asked him: "What was it I said that induced you to be a Christian?"

Said the young man: "Nothing that I have ever heard you say, but it is the way my mother lived." I tell you an ounce of example outweighs forty million tons of theory and speculation.

If the mothers would live as they should, we preachers would have little to do. Keep the devil out of the boys and girls and he will get out of the world. The old sinners will die off if we keep the young ones clean. The biggest place in the world is that which is being filled by the people who are closely in touch with youth. Being a king, an emperor or a president is mighty small potatoes compared to being a mother or the teacher of children, whether in a public school or in a Sunday school, and they fill places so great that there isn't an angel in Heaven that wouldn't be glad to give a bushel of diamonds to boot to come down here and take their places.

Commanding an army is little more than sweeping a street or pounding an anvil compared with the training of a boy or girl. The mother of Moses did more for the world than all the kings that Egypt ever had. To teach a child to love truth and hate a lie, to love purity and hate vice, is greater than inventing a flying machine that will take you to the moon before breakfast. Unconsciously you set in motion influences that will damn or bless the old universe and bring new worlds out of chaos and transform them to God.

A man sent a friend of mine some crystals from the Scientific American and said: "One of these crystals as large as a pin point will give a distinguishable green hue to 116 hogsheads of water." Think of it! Power enough in an atom to tincture 116 hogsheads of water. There is power in a word or act to blight a boy, and through him, curse a community. There is power enough in a word to tincture the life of that child so it will become a power to lift the world to Jesus Christ. The mother will put in motion influence that will either touch Heaven or Hell. Talk about greatness!

Oh, you wait until you reach the mountains of eternity, then read the mothers' names in God's hall of fame, and see what they have been in the world. Wait until you see God's hall of fame; you won't see any Ralph Waldo Emersons, but you will see women bent over the washtub. I want to tell you women, fooling away your time, hugging and kissing a poodle dog, caressing a "Spitz," drinking society brandy mash and a cocktail, and playing cards, is mighty small business compared to molding the life of a child.

Tell me, where did Moses get his faith? From his mother. Where did Moses get his backbone to say "I won't be called the son of Pharaoh's daughter"? He got it from his mother. Where did Moses get the nerve to say, "Excuse me, please", to the pleasure of Egypt? He got it from his mother.

You can bank on it that he didn't inhale it from his dad. Many a boy would have turned out better if his old dad had died before the kid was born. You tell your boy to keep out of bad company. Sometimes when he walks down the street with his father, he's in the worst company in town.

His dad smokes, drinks and chews. I would not clean his old spittoon. Let the hog clean his own trough. Moses got it from his ma. He was learned in all the wisdom of Egypt, but that didn't give him the swelled head.

When God wants to throw a world out into space, He is not concerned about it. The first mile that world takes settles its course for eternity. When God throws a child out into the world He is mighty anxious that it gets a right start.

The Catholics are right when they say: "Give us the children until they are 10 years old and we don't care who has them after that." The Catholics are not losing any sleep about losing men and women from their church membership. It is the only church that has ever shown us the only sensible way to reach the masses - that is, by getting hold of the children.

That's the only way on God's earth that you will ever solve the problem of reaching the masses. You get the boys and girls started right and the devil will hang a crepe on his door, bank his fires and Hell will be for rent before the Fourth of July.

A friend of mine has a little girl that she was compelled to take to the hospital for an operation. They thought she would be frightened, but she said: "I don't care if mamma will he there and hold my hand."

They prepared her for the operation, led her into the room, put her on the table, put the cone over her face and saturated it with ether, and she said, "Now, mamma, take me by the hand and hold it and I'll not be afraid".

And the mother stood there and held her hand. The operation was performed, and when she regained consciousness they said: "Bessie, weren't you afraid when they put you on the table?" She said: "No, mamma stood there and held my hand. I wasn't afraid."

There is a mighty power in a mother's hand. There's more power in a woman's hand than there is in a king's scepter. And there is a mighty power in a mother's kiss - inspiration, courage, hope, ambition, in a mother's kiss. One kiss made Benjamin West a painter, and the memory of it clung to him through life. One kiss will drive away the fear in the dark and make the little one brave. It will give strength where there is weakness.

I was in a town one day and saw a mother out with her boy, and he had great steel braces on both legs, to his hips, and when I got near enough to them I learned by their conversation that wasn't the first time the mother had had him out for a walk.

She had him out exercising him so he would get use of his limbs. He was struggling and she smiled and said: "You are doing fine today; better than you did yesterday," and she stooped and kissed him, and the kiss of encouragement made him work all the harder, and she said: "You are doing great, son," and he said, "Mamma, I'm going to run: look at me." And one of his toes caught on the steel brace on the other leg and he stumbled, but she caught him and kissed him, and said: "That was fine, son; how well you did it!"

Now, he did it because his mother had encouraged him with a kiss. He didn't do it to show off. There is nothing that will help and inspire like a mother's kiss.

If we knew the baby fingers pressed
against the window pane,
Would be cold and still tomorrow, never
trouble us again,
Would the bright eyes of our darling catch
the frown upon our brow?
Let us gather up the sunbeams lying all
around our path.
Let us keep the wheat and roses, casting
out the thorns and chaff!
We shall find our sweetest comforts in the
blessing of today,
With a patient hand removing all the briers
from our way.

There is power in a mother's song, too. It's the best music the world ever heard. The best music in the world is like biscuits - it's the kind mother makes. There is no brass band or pipe organ that can hold a candle to mother's song. Calve, Melba, Nordica, Eames, SchumannHeink - they are cheap skates compared to mother. They can't sing at all.

They don't know the rudiments of the kind of music mother sings. The kind she sings gets tangled up in your heart strings. There would be a disappointment in the music of Heaven to me if there were no mothers there to sing. The song of an angel or a seraph would not have much charm for me. What would you care for an angel's song if there is no mother's song? The song of a mother is sweeter than that ever sung by minstrel or written by poet. Talk about sonnets! You ought to hear the mother sing when her babe is on her breast, when her heart is filled with emotions. Her voice may not please an artist, but it will please anyone who has a heart in him. The songs that have moved the world are not the songs written by the great masters. The best music, in my judgment, is not the faultless rendition of these high priced opera singers.

There is nothing in art that can put into melody the happiness which associations and memories bring. I think when we reach heaven it will be found that some of the best songs we will sing there will be those we learned at mother's knee.

There is power in a mother's love. A mother's love must be like God's love. How God could ever tell the world that He loved it without a mother's help has often puzzled me. If the devils in Hell ever turned pale it was the day mother's love flamed up for the first time in a woman's heart. If the devil ever got "cold feet" it was that day, in my judgment. You know a mother has to love her babe before it is born. Like God, she has to go into the shadows of the valley of death to bring it into the world, and she will love her child, suffer for it and it can grow up and become vile and yet she will love it.

Nothing will make her blame it, and I think, women, that one of the awful things in Hell will be that there will be no mother's love there. Nothing but black, bottomless, endless, eternal hate in Hell - no mother's love.

And though he creep through the vilest caves of sin,
And crouch perhaps, with bleared and bloodshot eyes,
Under the hangman's rope - a mother's lips
Will kiss him in his last bed of disgrace,
And love him e'en for what she hoped of him.

I thank God for what mother's love has done for the world. Oh, there is power in a mother's trust. Surely as Moses was put in his mother's arms by the princess, so God put the babes in your arms, as a charge by him to raise and care for. Every child is put in a mother's arms as a trust from God, and she has to answer to God for the way she deals with that child. No mother on God's earth has any right to raise her children for pleasure. She has no right to send them to dancing school and haunts of sin. You have no right to do those things that will curse your children. That babe is put in your arms to train for the Lord. No mother has any more right to raise her children for pleasure than I have to pick your pockets or throw red pepper in your eyes. She has no more right to do that than a bank cashier has to rifle the vaults and take the savings of the people. One of the worst sins you can commit is to be unfaithful to your trust. "Take this child and nurse it for me". That is all the business you have with it. That is a jewel that belongs to God and He gives it to you to polish for Him so He can set it in a crown. Who knows but Judas became the godless, good-for-nothing wretch he was because he had a godless, good-for-nothing mother? Do you know? I don't.

Who is more to blame for the crowded prisons than mothers? Who is more to blame for the crowded, disreputable houses than you are, to let your children gad the streets with every Tom, Dick and Harry, or keep company with some little jack rabbit whose character would make a black mark on a piece of tar paper. I have talked with men in prisons who have damned their mothers to their face. Why? They blame their mothers for their being where they are.

"Take the child and nurse it for me, and I will pay you your wages." God pays in joy that is fireproof, famine proof and devil proof. He will pay you, don't you worry. So get your name on God's payroll. "Take this child and nurse it for Me, and I will pay you your wages."

If you haven't been doing that, then get your name on God's payroll. You have been drawing wages from the devil. Why have you a bleary eyed, sickly, cigarette smoking boy? Why have you a girl whose reputation is kicked around like a football? Why? You have been working for the devil, and see what you have.

"Take this child and nurse it for me, and I will pay you your wages". Then your responsibility! It is so great that I don't see how any woman can fail to be a Christian and serve God. What do you think God will do if the mother fails? I stagger under it. What if, through your unfaithfulness, your boy becomes a curse and your daughter a blight? What, if through your neglect, that boy becomes a Judas, when he might have been a John or Paul?

Down in Cincinnati some years ago a mother went to the zoological garden and stood leaning over the bear pit, watching the bears and dropping crumbs and peanuts to them. In her arms she held her babe, a year and three months old. She was so interested in the bears that the baby wriggled itself out of her arms and she watched those huge monsters rip it to shreds. What a veritable Hell it will be all through her life to know that her little one was lost through her own carelessness and neglect!

"Take this child and raise it for me, and I will pay you your wages." Will you promise and covenant with God, and with me, and with one another, that from now on you will try, with God's help, to do better than you ever have done to raise your children for God?